HOUGHTON MIFFLIN HARCOURT

Tennessee Science

Interactive Workbook and TCAP Practice

HOUGHTON MIFFLIN HARCOURT
School Publishers

Printed in the U.S.A.

ISBN: 978-0-547-18143-1

8 9 10-0877-17 16 15 14 13   4500419023

Contents

Contents

Contents

What Do You Know?

Talk with a partner.

List different plants you know.

What parts do these plants have?

_____

_____

_____

  Visit www.eduplace.com/tnscp to learn more.

Plants Are Living Things

Contents

What Do You Want to Know?

What do you wonder about how plants grow?

_____

_____

_____

_____

_____

5

VOCABULARY

living thing Something that grows and changes. *(noun)*

nutrient A material in soil that helps a plant live and grow. *(noun)*

shelter A place where a living thing can be safe. *(noun)*

VOCABULARY ACTIVITY

Use Syllables

nutrient

Break the word **nutrient** into syllables.
Say each syllable aloud.
Clap once for each syllable.
How many syllables are in **nutrient**?

GLE 0207.1.1 Recognize that plants and animals are made up of smaller parts and use food, water, and air to survive.

GLE 0207.5.1 Investigate the relationship between an animal's characteristics and the features of the environment where it lives.

6

1 How Are the Needs of Living Things Different?

A **living thing** is something that grows and changes.
Living things make other living things that are like them.
Plants and animals are living things.

Big trees need more water and room to grow than small flowers need.

All living things need air and food.
They also need water and room
to grow.
A large animal needs more air,
food, water, and room than a small
animal needs.
A large plant needs more air,
food, water, and room than a small
plant needs.

**These flowers are
living things.**

1. (Circle) the things that living things
   need to grow.

2. A large plant needs _____
   food, air, and room than a smaller
   plant.

3. What do plants and animals need?

Plants   **Animals**

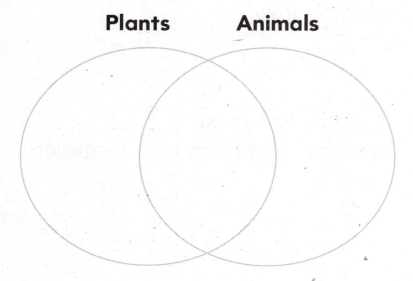

Animals also need shelter.
A **shelter** is a place where a living thing can be safe.
A big animal needs a big shelter.
A small animal needs a small shelter.

A hummingbird is small.
It needs a small shelter.

Many animals use plants for shelter.
Some animals use a hole in a tree
for shelter.
Others find shelter under roots
or leaves.
Some animals find shelter
in the water.
Others find shelter under rocks
and logs.
Shelters help keep animals from
getting hurt.

**An eagle needs a bigger shelter than
a hummingbird.**

4. Where do animals find shelter?

_____

_____

_____

I Wonder . . . Animals need
shelter. Which animals find shelter
under rocks or logs?

_____

See page 216 for the Express Lab.

 0207.2.1

Circle the correct answer.

5. **What happens when plants do not get water?**

Ⓐ They grow.

Ⓑ They die.

Ⓒ There is no change.

GLE 0207.1.1

10

What Plants Need

Plants do not move from place to place like animals do.
Plants must get everything they need where they grow.

These sunflowers are getting what they need to live.

Plants are living things.
They need air, food, water, and room to grow.
Plants that do not get what they need may die.

This plant is not getting enough water.

6. Look at the plant on this page. List what the plant needs to be healthy. Draw the healthy plant.

_____

_____

7. Why do plants need the Sun?

_____

_____

_____

8. Circle what plants use to make their own food.

Plants also need light from the Sun. Light from the Sun helps plants grow. Plants do not get food like other living things do. Plants make their own food. They use light from the Sun, air, water, and nutrients.

A **nutrient** is a material in the ground that helps a plant live and grow.
Plants also get water from the ground.
Plants use the food that they make to grow and change.

The tree gets water and nutrients from the ground.

Summary

Living things need food, water, air, and room to grow.
What do plants get from the ground?

_____

_____

▶ ## Main Idea

What do plants need to live?

Plants need things to live.

Main Idea

What do plants need to live?

13

VOCABULARY

flower The plant part where fruit and seeds form. *(noun)*

fruit The part of a flower that grows around a seed. *(noun)*

seed The part from which a new plant grows. *(noun)*

VOCABULARY ACTIVITY

Use Pictures

fruit

Look at the picture of the fruit on this page.
What do you know about fruit from the picture?

_____

_____

14   **GLE 0207.1.1** Recognize that plants and animals are made up of smaller parts and use food, water, and air to survive.

2 How Do Plants Meet Their Needs?

A plant has many parts.
A plant's parts help it grow and change.
Some parts help a plant make new plants.
A **flower** is where fruit and seeds come from.
A **fruit** is the part that grows around a seed.
A **seed** is the part from which a new plant grows.

seed

flower

fruit

Some parts help a plant get food. First the parts help the plant get what it needs to make food. Then the parts help move the food through the plant.

Stems carry water and nutrients from one part of a plant to another.

Leaves take in light, air and water to make food.

Roots take in water and nutrients from the ground. Roots also hold the plant in place.

The food moves from the leaves to other parts of the plant.

I. List the parts of a plant.

_____

_____

3. How do plants use their stems?

_____

_____

_____

I Wonder . . . Plants need sunlight. How do plants that do not get much sunlight stay healthy?

_____

_____

_____

How Plants Use Their Parts

All plants have roots, stems, and leaves.

The roots, stems, and leaves are not the same on every plant.

The trunk of a tree is a stem.

It grows tall so leaves get light from the Sun.

The stem of a cactus stores water.

Thorns on some stems keep animals away.

A **rosebush** has stems with thorns that keep some animals away.

Some plants have roots that spread out in the ground.
Their long roots can get water from all around.
Some trees have long roots.
Their roots help them live in many places.

This water lily has a long stem. It goes all the way to the bottom of the pond.

Compare

How are all plants alike?

Summary

A plant's parts help it to grow and change. List the plant parts and their uses.

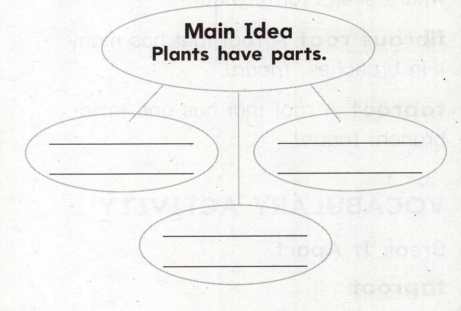

Main Idea
Plants have parts.

▶ Compare

How are all plants alike?

_____

_____

VOCABULARY

cone A part of a nonflowering plant where seeds form. (*noun*)

fibrous root A root that has many thin branches. (*noun*)

taproot A root that has one main branch. (*noun*)

VOCABULARY ACTIVITY

Break It Apart

taproot

Write the two smaller words in **taproot.**

_____

_____

GLE 0207.1.1 Recognize that plants and animals are made up of smaller parts and use food, water, and air to survive.

3 How Can Plants Be Grouped?

There are many kinds of plants. Plants can be grouped by their parts. One group of plants has flowers. Another group of plants has cones.

Flowers and Cones

flower

A flower is where the fruit and seeds come from.
A **cone** is a part of a plant that has no flowers.
It is where the seeds come from.
The cone protects the seeds.

cones

1. One way to group plants is by their _____ or _____.

2. Draw a plant with flowers.
Draw a plant with cones.

I Wonder . . . Plants can be grouped by their stems. What are other ways to group plants?

_____

_____

_____

3. What are some stems that we might eat?

_____

4. Put an X on the stems shown on this page.

Plants can be grouped by their stems.
Many flowers and vegetables have soft, green stems.
Many bushes and trees have stems that are hard.
We eat the stems of some plants.
Broccoli and celery are stems that we eat.

soft, green stem

hard stem

Plants can be grouped by their leaves.
Many trees and small plants have wide, flat leaves.
Many trees with cones have leaves that look like needles.
Pine, fir, and spruce trees have these leaves.

wide, flat leaf

leaves that look like needles

Circle the correct answer.

5. Trees with cones likely have leaves that are

Ⓐ wide

Ⓑ flat

Ⓒ needles

GLE 0207.1.1

21

6. Circle the meaning of **taproot**.

7. Draw a plant with a taproot.

Kinds of Roots

Plants can be grouped by their roots.
A **taproot** is a root that has one main branch.
We eat some roots, such as carrots.

taproot

A **fibrous root** is a root that has many thin branches.

fibrous root

Classify

What is one way that plants can be grouped?

Summary

Scientists group plants by their parts. How can you group plants by their roots?

_____

_____

 ## Classify

What is one way that plants can be grouped?

Stems	Leaves

VOCABULARY

life cycle The series of changes that a living thing goes through as it grows. *(noun)*

seedling A young plant that grows from a seed. *(noun)*

VOCABULARY ACTIVITY

life cycle

Look at the pictures of the tomato plant shown on these pages.

What do you know about a **life cycle** from these pictures?

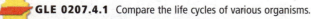

GLE 0207.4.1 Compare the life cycles of various organisms.

GLE 0207.4.2 Realize that parents pass along physical characteristics to their offspring.

4 How Do Plants Change During Their Life Cycles?

All living things grow, change, and die.

The number of changes that a living thing goes through is its **life cycle**.

All plants are not the same.

They may have different life cycles.

Most plants start from a seed.

The seed sprouts when it gets what it needs.

The young plant is called a **seedling**.

The plant grows and makes flowers.

Seeds   A seedling

The seedling grows and changes.
It grows flowers that make seeds.
New plants can grow from
these seeds.
These plants will look like the plant
that dropped the seeds.
The cycle of growing and changing
starts again.

Flowers make fruit. Seeds grow inside the fruit. Then the plant dies. The seeds fall. They may grow into new plants.

_____

_____

_____

_____

TCAP Practice

Circle the correct answer.

The _____ makes seeds.

(A) flower

(B) leaf

(C) stem

GLE 0207.1.1

25

Summary

Plants grow and change in different ways. How do tomato plants change?

_____

_____

▶ Sequence

When does a young plant sprout?

A young plant sprouts…

↓

The Same but Different

Acorns are the fruit of an oak tree.
Acorns fall to the ground.
Then the seeds inside may grow
new plants.
The seedlings may not be the same
size or shape.
But the seedlings grow into the
same kind of tree.

oak tree

seedlings

acorns

Sequence

When does a young plant sprout?

26

KWL

What Did You Learn?

🍂 **TCAP Practice**

❶ A _____ is the part of a flower that grows around a seed.

Ⓐ stem

Ⓑ fruit

Ⓒ leaf

GLE 0207.1.1

❷ What four things do all living things need?

❸ Which kind of root has one main branch?

❹ How can you tell when a plant near your home is not getting what it needs?

KWL

What Did You Learn?

🍂 **TCAP Practice**

❶ Circle the correct answer.

❷ Living things need _____, _____, _____, and _____.

❸ A _____ has one main branch.

❹ The plant near my home is not getting what it needs because

_____

_____

 the correct answer.

1 **How do roots help plants meet their needs?**

  Ⓐ They carry nutrients from one part of the plant to another.

  Ⓑ They hold the plant in place.

  Ⓒ They take in light, air, and water.

GLE 0207.1.1

2 **What will happen if you plant the seeds from a tomato?**

  Ⓐ They will grow into plants that will be the same size.

  Ⓑ They will grow into plants with the same number of leaves.

  Ⓒ They will grow into tomato plants.

3 **Look at the picture.**

Why is a pine cone important to a pine tree?

  Ⓐ It protects the tree's seeds.

  Ⓑ It becomes a flower.

  Ⓒ It connects the roots of the tree with the leaves.

 GLE 0207.1.1

GLE 0207.4.2

4 **Which picture shows a seedling?**

Ⓐ

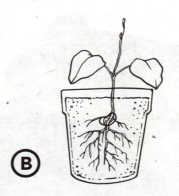

Ⓑ

Ⓒ

GLE 0207.4.1

5 **How does the long stem of a water lily help it live in a pond?**

Ⓐ The stem connects the roots at the bottom of the pond with the leaf at the top.

Ⓑ The stem takes in water from the pond and carries the water to the roots.

Ⓒ The stem makes food from water, air, and sunlight and feeds the plant.

0207.2.2

6 **How are plants different from animals?**

Ⓐ Plants need air and water.

Ⓑ Plants make their own food.

Ⓒ Plants are made up of smaller parts.

GLE 0207.1.1

KWL.

What Do You Know?

Talk with a partner.

Make a list of animals that you know.

_____

_____

_____

_____

_____

_____

_____

Animal Life Cycles

Go Digital Visit www.eduplace.com/tnscp to learn more.

Contents

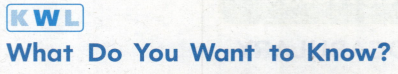

What Do You Want to Know?

What do you wonder about animals?

_____

_____

_____

_____

_____

_____

VOCABULARY

adaptation A body part or action that helps a living thing meet its needs where it lives. *(noun)*

VOCABULARY ACTIVITY

Use Words

adaptation

Some words on this page help you know what **adaptation** means. (Circle) them.

GLE 0207.1.1 Recognize that plants and animals are made up of smaller parts and use food, water, and air to survive.

1 How Do Animals Meet Their Needs?

Sometimes animals are not able to get what they need to live. Then they have to move or their bodies need to change. An **adaptation** is a body part or action that helps a living thing meet its needs where it lives.

Meeting Needs on Land

Some adaptations help animals meet their needs on land. Strong legs and sharp claws are two kinds of adaptations.

Leopard

strong legs

sharp claws

Meeting Needs in Water

Other adaptations help animals meet their needs in water.
Fins or flippers help animals move in water.
Special mouth parts help animals eat.

mouth

Manta Ray

large, flat fins

1. What adaptation does a giraffe have?

_____

_____

TCAP Practice

Circle the correct answer.

2. What are adaptations of animals that live in water?

Ⓐ fins

Ⓑ strong legs

Ⓒ wings

GLE 0207.1.1

Express Lab

See page 217 for the Express Lab.

0207.3.1

Summary

Animals have adaptations that help them stay alive. What adaptations does a bird have?

 Draw Conclusions

Why do different animals have different adaptations?

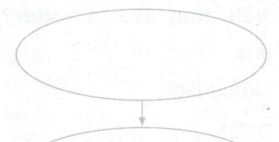

Animals have different adaptations.

Meeting Needs in Air

Birds have adaptations that help them fly.
A bird's feathers help it move and fly.
Its tail helps, too.
Birds also have hollow bones that are strong and light.

Red-tailed Hawk

wings

tail

Draw Conclusions

Why do different animals have different adaptations?

Which Baby Animals Look Like Their Parents?

All living things grow.
All living things change.
All living things reproduce.
When living things **reproduce**, they make more living things of the same kind.
Things that are not living do not reproduce.

VOCABULARY

 offspring The group of living things that come from the same living thing. *(noun)*

reproduce To make more living things of the same kind. *(verb)*

 = Tennessee Academic Vocabulary

VOCABULARY ACTIVITY

Break It Apart

offspring

Write the two smaller words in **offspring**.

_____

_____

 GLE 0207.4.1 Compare the life cycles of various organisms.

GLE 0207.4.2 Realize that parents pass along physical characteristics to their offspring.

35

1. Living things come from _____

_____.

2. Draw a line to match the parent with its offspring.

dog   fawn

deer   kitten

cat   foal

horse   puppy

All living things come from other living things.

Offspring are the group of living things that come from the same living thing.

Children are the offspring of their parents.

Kittens are the offspring of their parents.

Kittens are all young cats.
Kittens born together are the same in some ways.
They are different in some ways, too.
Their fur can be different colors.

3. List three ways one of the kittens looks like its parent.

_____

_____

_____

4. List three ways the kittens look different from each other.

_____

_____

_____

I Wonder . . . Birds are hatched from eggs. How does a baby bird change as it grows?

_____

_____

_____

Familiar Life Cycles

Different kinds of animals grow in different ways.
Their life cycles are different.
Birds have young that look like their parents.

Life Cycle of a Bird

A mother bird lays eggs. A baby bird grows inside each egg.

A baby comes out of the egg. A parent feeds it.

The young bird grows up. It can reproduce.

The baby bird gets new feathers as it grows.

(Circle) the correct answer.

5. Which do baby birds look like?

(A) eggs

(B) kittens

(C) their parents

GLE 0207.4.2

6. How does the parent bird care for its offspring?

_____

_____

_____

_____

7. How does a baby mouse change as it grows?

_____

_____

_____

8. Circle the adult mice shown on these pages.

Mice have young that look like their parents, too.

Life Cycle of a Mouse

A mother mouse gives birth to baby mice.

The mother mouse makes milk for her babies. The babies drink the milk.

The young mouse grows up.
It can reproduce.

The babies
grow more fur.
They get bigger.

Compare and Contrast

How is the life cycle of a bird
different from that of a mouse?

Summary

Animals grow and change during their life cycles. Many animals of the same kind look like their parents. What baby animals do you know that look like their parents?

_____

_____

 ## Compare and Contrast

How is the life cycle of a bird different from that of a mouse?

Bird	Mouse

VOCABULARY

larva The worm-like stage in an insect's life cycle. (*noun*)

pupa The stage when an insect changes form. (*noun*)

VOCABULARY ACTIVITY

Use Pictures

larva

Turn the page to look at the picture of the larva.
Describe how the larva looks.

_____

_____

 GLE 0207.4.1 Compare the life cycles of various organisms.

GLE 0207.4.2 Realize that parents pass along physical characteristics to their offspring.

3 Which Baby Animals Do Not Look Like Their Parents?

Some baby animals do not look like their parents.
Young amphibians look different from their parents.
When they grow up, they will look like their parents.

Life Cycle of a Frog

A frog lays its eggs in water.

Tadpoles come out of the eggs. They have gills and a tail, but no legs.

A frog is an amphibian.

When frogs come out of eggs, they have body parts that help them live in water.

Then they grow parts that help them live on land.

Parts that they needed to live in water disappear.

When they grow up, they will look like their parents.

An adult frog can reproduce.

A tadpole grows back legs.

Lungs grow. Gills disappear. The tail will soon disappear, too.

1. Number the correct order of the life cycle of a frog.

_____ _____ _____

2. Compare an adult frog to a young frog.

_____

_____

_____

43

3. (Circle) the larva on this page.

4. How does this insect change form as it grows?

_____

_____

_____

_____

Life Cycle of a Butterfly

Butterflies belong to an animal group called insects.
Most insects change form as they grow.
A butterfly lays eggs on a plant.
A larva comes out of an egg.
A **larva** looks like a worm.
The larva eats the plant.

butterfly egg

This pupa's wings and legs are growing.

larva

A larva grows and turns into a pupa.
A **pupa** is when the insect changes form.
A pupa does not eat.

**A butterfly lives for several weeks.
It lays eggs. Then a new cycle starts.**

The change is done. The pupa is now a butterfly.

Circle the correct answer.

5. **Which stage comes before the pupa stage in an insect's life cycle?**

   (A) adult

   (B) larva

   (C) egg

   GLE 0207.4.1

I Wonder . . . Frogs and butterflies hatch from eggs. The offspring look different from their parents.
What other animals that hatch from eggs look like their parents?

_____

_____

45

6. A larva is one stage in the life cycle of a dragonfly.

How is the larva of a dragonfly different from the larva of a butterfly?

_____

_____

7. (Circle) the parts a dragonfly uses to fly.

Life Cycle of a Dragonfly

A dragonfly is an insect.
It changes during its life cycle, too.
A dragonfly lays eggs in or near the water.
The larva uses gills to breathe.
It changes its skin as it grows.

egg

larva

It grows parts to help it live on land.
It grows parts to fly in the air.
It comes out of the water.
It is now a dragonfly.

Summary

Animals grow and change during their life cycles. Frogs and butterflies do not look like their parents when they are born. What other animals do not look like their parents when they are born?

_____

_____

 ## Sequence

What happens to a frog after parts for living on land form?

A frog grows legs and lungs.

↓

_____

Sequence

What happens to a frog after parts for living on land form?

47

Chapter 2 Review

TCAP Practice

❶ (Circle) the correct answer.

❷ A dragonfly's life cycle _____

_____

❸ Cat offspring are alike _____

_____

Cat offspring are different _____

_____

❹ A frog _____

_____

48

TCAP Practice

❶ What is the group of living things that come from the same living thing?

Ⓐ reproduce

Ⓑ offspring

Ⓒ larva

GLE 0207.4.2

❷ How is a dragonfly's life cycle different from a butterfly's life cycle?

❸ How are cat offspring alike and different?

❹ How are the life cycles of a frog and a butterfly different?

Draw an animal's life cycle.

Circle the correct answer.

1 **Which animal looks like its parents when it is very young?**

(A) butterfly

(B) bird

(C) dragonfly

GLE 0207.4.2

2 **Fins help fish**

(A) move in water

(B) catch food

(C) breathe in water

GLE 0207.1.1

3 **Look at the picture.**

What happens next in this animal's life cycle?

(A)

(B)

(C)

GLE 0207.4.1

4 How do lions use claws to help them meet their needs?

Ⓐ Claws help them breathe air.

Ⓑ Claws help them catch food.

Ⓒ Claws help them drink. 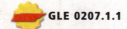 GLE 0207.1.1

5 Look at the picture.

What will be true of __all__ of the offspring of this cat?

Ⓐ They will all have striped fur.

Ⓑ They will all be kittens.

Ⓒ They will all be the same size.

 GLE 0207.4.2

6 Which animal has adaptations that allow it to fly?

Ⓐ

Ⓑ

Ⓒ

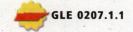 GLE 0207.1.1

What Do You Know?

List environments you know.

Pick one environment.

What kind of plants and animals live there?

_____

_____

_____

_____

_____

_____

Environments

Go Digital Visit www.eduplace.com/tnscp to learn more.

Contents

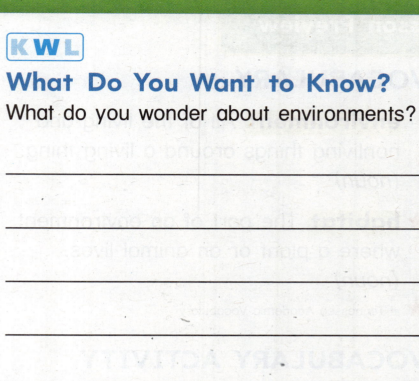

What Do You Want to Know?

What do you wonder about environments?

_____

_____

_____

_____

_____

_____

_____

_____

_____

_____

_____

VOCABULARY

environment All of the living and nonliving things around a living thing. *(noun)*

★ **habitat** The part of an environment where a plant or an animal lives. *(noun)*

★ = Tennessee Academic Vocabulary

VOCABULARY ACTIVITY

Use Syllables

environment

Break the word **environment** into syllables.

Say each syllable out loud.

How many syllables are in the word **environment?**

GLE 0207.2.2 Investigate living things found in different places.

1 What Makes Up an Environment?

All the living and nonliving things around a living thing make up an **environment**.
Plants and animals are living things. Soil and water are nonliving things. Rocks and air are nonliving things.

The world has many kinds of environments.
Different plants and animals live in each one.
They adapt to the environment where they live.
An alpine tundra is cold and dry.
Plants grow low to the ground to be safe from the wind.

Alpine Tundra

1. List the living and nonliving things in an environment.

Living	Nonliving

2. Describe an alpine tundra.

_____

_____

_____

_____

I Wonder . . . Rain forests are wet environments. Which living things might live in a rain forest?

_____

_____

_____

3. What nonliving things are found in a rain forest?

_____

_____

_____

An environment can be hot or cold.
It can be wet or dry.
Some environments have many trees and plants.
A rain forest is a warm and wet place.
It has many kinds of plants.

Rain Forest

Other environments have very few plants.
A prairie is hot in the summer.
It is cold in the winter.

Prairie

4. Circle the words that describe the prairie.

5. Draw an animal that lives in a prairie environment.

6. How are rain forests, prairies, and water environments alike?

_____

_____

_____

7. Why does a fish live in a water habitat?

_____

_____

_____

_____

Express Lab

See page 218 for the Express Lab.

✔ 0207.1.1

Meeting Needs

Living things will keep living if they get what they need. Different plants and animals live in different environments. A **habitat** is the part of an environment where a plant or an animal lives.

A fish lives in a water habitat.

It is hot in a desert.
Animals find shelter under rocks.
Animals find shelter under the ground.
They look for food at night, when it is cool.
Many desert animals get water from the foods they eat.

A cactus has a thick stem that holds water.

The lizard has spotted skin. This helps it hide.

Circle the correct answer.

8. What type of environment does a cactus live in?

(A) ocean

(B) rain forest

(C) desert

GLE 0207.2.2

9. Draw a desert environment. Show living and nonliving things found there.

59

10. Draw an animal.
Label the body part that it uses to get food.

Plants have parts that help them live in their habitats.
Animals do, too.
Some parts help them stay safe.
Other parts help them get food and water.

Raccoons use long, sharp claws to catch food.

claws

This bird lives in a rain forest.
It has a large beak.
The beak helps the bird get food.
These goats live in the tundra.
Their hooves help them climb
the rocks.

beak

hooves

Main Idea

What are three different kinds
of environments?

Summary

Living things get what they need from
their environment.
How do birds get what they need from a
rain forest?

_____

_____

Main Idea

What are three different kinds of
environments?

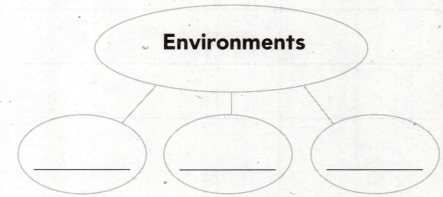

Environments

VOCABULARY

stream A small river. (noun)

VOCABULARY ACTIVITY

Use Pictures

stream

Look at the picture of the **stream** on this page.

What do you know about this **stream**?

_____

_____

_____

GLE 0207.2.1 Investigate the habitats of different kinds of local plants and animals.

62

GLE 0207.2.2 Investigate living things found in different places.

2 What Is a Stream Habitat?

A **stream** is a small river. The stream and everything around it make up a stream habitat. Many living things are in a stream habitat. Many nonliving things are in a stream habitat.

A stream habitat has plants and animals. It has air and water. It has rocks and dirt.

A stream habitat meets the needs of many living things.
Plants get water from the stream.
Animals use water from the stream, too.
Plants and animals use the air.
Fish live in the stream.
Fish eat plants and insects that live in the water.

Small animals can hide in the rocks found by a stream.

I. Circle the nonliving things shown on these pages.

I Wonder . . . There are many living things in a stream habitat. What lives in a stream?

_____

_____

_____

_____

Circle the correct answer.

2. What body part does a fish use to move in a stream?

Ⓐ gills

Ⓑ fins

Ⓒ lungs

GLE 0207.2.2

3. What adaptation do floating plants have that help them survive in a stream?

_____

_____

_____

64

Life in a Stream

Living things in a stream habitat have special parts called adaptations. These adaptations help them meet their needs. Plants that float have roots that hang in the water. A fish uses fins to swim. It uses gills to get air from the water.

fish

gills

fin

roots

A heron is a bird with long legs.
It uses its long legs to walk in the water.

frog

turtle

heron

plants that float

Draw Conclusions

What nonliving things in a stream habitat do animals use?

Summary

A stream is a small river.
What living and nonliving things are found in and around a stream?

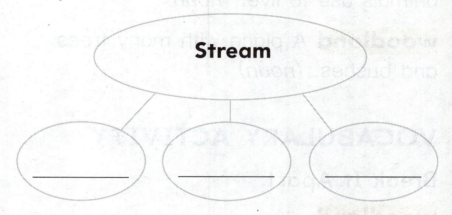

Stream

▶ **Draw Conclusions**   What nonliving things in a stream habitat do animals use?

_____

_____

VOCABULARY

resource Something that plants and animals use to live. *(noun)*

woodland A place with many trees and bushes. *(noun)*

VOCABULARY ACTIVITY

Break It Apart

woodland

Write the two smaller words in **woodland.**

_____ _____

GLE **0207.2.2** Investigate living things found in different places.

GLE **0207.5.1** Investigate the relationship between an animal's characteristics and the features of the environment where it lives.

3 What Is a Woodland Habitat?

A **woodland** is a place with many trees and bushes. Living things in a woodland habitat have adaptations. These adaptations help them stay alive.

Many woodland animals have parts that help them climb trees.
Many have parts that help them fly.
Many woodland animals are brown. This color helps them hide.

hawk

squirrel

fox

I Wonder . . . Animals have adaptations that allow them to live in different places. What adaptations does a hawk have that keep it safe in a woodland habitat?

_____

_____

TCAP Practice

Circle the correct answer.

1. Which adaptation does a fox have?

   (A) color that helps it hide

   (B) parts that help it climb trees

   (C) parts that help it fly

GLE 0207.2.2

67

2. How are trees a resource for birds?

_____

_____

_____

Trees Are Resources

A **resource** is something that plants and animals use to live.
A tree is a resource.
A tree can give living things food.
A tree can give living things shelter.

A bird and an insect can find food in a tree.

bark

branch

An owl and a squirrel use a tree for shelter.

Animals use all parts of a tree. They use the roots, leaves, and nuts for food. Some animals build nests in tree branches. Others live on leaves or under the bark.

Compare and Contrast

How do animals use trees to meet their needs?

Summary

A woodland is a place with many trees and bushes. Animals have adaptations to survive in a woodland. Compare the adaptations of an owl and a fox.

Owl	Fox

 ## Compare and Contrast

How do animals use trees to meet their needs?

_____

_____

69

VOCABULARY

energy The ability to do things. *(noun)*

food chain The order in which energy passes from one living thing to another. *(noun)*

food web A model that shows how different food chains are related. *(noun)*

VOCABULARY ACTIVITY

Use Pictures

food chain

Turn the page to look at the pictures of a **food chain.**

What do you know about a **food chain**?

_____

_____

GLE 0207.2.3 Identify basic ways that plants and animals depend on each other.

GLE 0207.3.1 Recognize that animals eat plants or other animals for food.

70

4 How Do Plants and Animals Get Energy?

You use energy when you run or play.
Energy is the ability to do things.
Living things get energy from food.
Plants are living things.
Plants use sunlight to make food.
The food gives them energy to grow and change.

Young wasps get energy by eating the hornworm.

Animals are living things, too.
Animals get energy from the food they eat.
They use the energy to grow and change.
Different animals eat different kinds of food.
Some animals eat only plants.
Some animals eat only other animals.
Some animals eat plants and other animals.

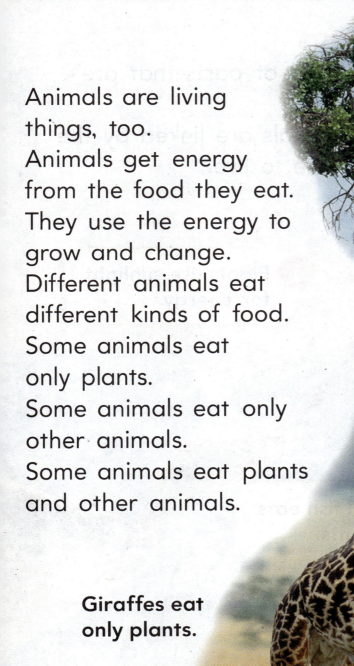

Giraffes eat only plants.

I Wonder . . . Some animals eat both other animals and plants. What animals eat only plants?

_____

_____

I. Animals get energy from _____

_____.

2. Why is the Sun important in this food chain?

_____

_____

_____

_____

3. What might small fish eat?

_____

_____

Food Chains

A chain is made of parts that are linked together.
Plants and animals are linked by the energy they use to live.

1 Plants use sunlight for energy.

2 A small fish eats the plants.

A **food chain** shows the order that energy moves from one living thing to another.
Look at the picture of a food chain.
It starts with the Sun.
The arrows show the order that energy moves.

3 A big fish eats the small fish.

5. Fill in the chart using the food chain shown on these two pages.

Sun
↓

↓

↓

Most food chains start with the Sun.
Most plants use sunlight to make food.
Food gives the plants energy.

Grass gets energy from the Sun.

A cow eats the grass.

Look at these pictures.
The arrows show how energy moves
in the food chain.

**People drink milk that
came from the cow.**

6. A rabbit eats grass.
Draw a food chain with a rabbit.

7. A food web shows _____

_____.

8. Circle the animals that the hawk eats.

Food Webs

There can be many food chains in one environment.

A **food web** shows how food chains are related.

Look at this picture.

It shows a food web made up of some desert food chains.

hawk

mouse

grass

One part of a food web may change.
The change may touch the lives of other living things in the web.
Their lives may change, too.

Sequence

With what do most food chains begin?

jackrabbit

snake

Summary

Living things get energy from food. Compare the food chain with the hawk to the food chain with the jackrabbit.

Hawk	Jackrabbit

▶ **Sequence** With what do most food chains begin?

_____

_____

77

What Did You Learn?

TCAP Practice

❶ (Circle) the correct answer.

❷ Fish _____ from a stream.

❸ Plants get energy from _____.
Animals get energy from
_____.

❹ Adaptations help animals
_____.

Responding

What Did You Learn?

TCAP Practice

❶ **A cactus grows well in a desert because it has**

Ⓐ no roots

Ⓑ a thick stem

Ⓒ bright colored flowers

GLE 0207.2.2

❷ How do fish use a stream to meet their needs?

❸ Describe how plants and animals get energy.

❹ How do adaptations help animals survive?

Draw a picture of an animal in its environment.

Circle the correct answer.

1 Which of the following is <u>not</u> a source of energy for animals?

Ⓐ air

Ⓑ plants

Ⓒ other animals

GLE 0207.3.1

2 What nonliving things are found in a Tennessee stream habitat?

Ⓐ insects

Ⓑ rocks

Ⓒ fish

GLE 0207.2.1

3 Which animal would <u>most likely</u> be found in a woodland habitat?

Ⓐ

Ⓑ

Ⓒ

GLE 0207.2.2

4 Look at the picture.

This animal __most likely__ lives where the ground is covered with

(A) grass

(B) snow

(C) rocks

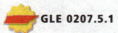 GLE 0207.5.1

5 Why do many plants live in a rain forest?

(A) It has a lot of water and is warm.

(B) It is very cold in the winter.

(C) It is very dry and windy.  GLE 0207.2.2

6 Look at the picture.

How is this plant a resource for animals?

(A) It can grow very tall.

(B) Insects can eat its leaves.

(C) It grows in woodland habitats.

GLE 0207.2.3

KWL

What Do You Know?

What do you know about Earth's resources?

Make a list of Earth's resources.

_____

_____

_____

_____

_____

_____

_____

_____

 Visit www.eduplace.com/tnscp to learn more.

Earth's Resources

Contents

What Do You Want to Know?

What do you wonder about Earth's resources and how we use them?

_____

_____

_____

_____

_____

_____

_____

VOCABULARY

humus Tiny bits of dead plants and animals in soil. *(noun)*

mineral A nonliving solid found on Earth. *(noun)*

rock A solid made of one or more minerals. *(noun)*

soil The loose material that covers Earth's surface. *(noun)*

VOCABULARY ACTIVITY

Use Words

mineral

Which words on this page help you know what **mineral** means?

Circle them.

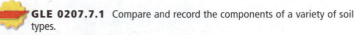

GLE 0207.7.1 Compare and record the components of a variety of soil types.

GLE 0207.7.2 Describe rocks according to their origin, size, shape, texture, and color.

84

1 What Makes Up Rocks and Soils?

Earth is made up of land and water. Earth's land is made of different kinds of solids.
A **mineral** is a nonliving solid found on Earth.
There are many kinds of minerals.

Rocks

A **rock** is a solid made of one or more minerals.
All rocks are not the same.
Rocks are different colors and sizes.
Different kinds of rocks are used in different ways.

Ways People Use Rocks

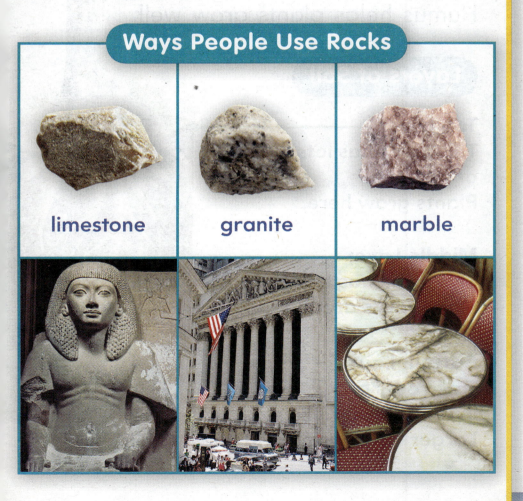

limestone   granite   marble

I. List different ways rocks can be used.

_____

_____

 See page 219 for the Express Lab.

0207.7.4

Circle the correct answer.

2. Humus is

Ⓐ dead plants and animals

Ⓑ air

Ⓒ bits of rock

GLE 0207.7.1

I Wonder . . . There are many layers of soil. Why do plants grow in the top layer of soil?

_____

_____

_____

Soils

Soil is the loose material that covers Earth's surface. There are bits of rock, humus, air, and water in soil. **Humus** is tiny bits of dead plants and animals in soil. Humus helps plants grow well.

Layers of Soil

Top Layer
This layer has lots of humus.
Plants grow here.

Middle Layer
This layer has less humus.
Small rocks are found here.

Bottom Layer
Tree roots grow down into this layer.
Larger rocks are found here.

Soil is important to all living things.
Plants get water and nutrients
from soil.
Animals get energy from plants.
Different plants grow better
in different kinds of soil.

clay soil

topsoil

Compare And Contrast

How are the three layers
of soil different?

Summary

The surface of the Earth is made of
different solid materials.
List the different solids.

Earth's surface is
made of solids.

 ## Compare and Contrast

How are the three layers of soil
different?

_____

_____

_____

_____

87

VOCABULARY

★ **natural resource** Something found in nature that people need or use. *(noun)*

nonrenewable resource A natural resource that cannot easily be replaced once it has been used. *(noun)*

renewable resource A natural resource that can be replaced by nature. *(noun)*

★ = Tennessee Academic Vocabulary

VOCABULARY ACTIVITY

Use Pictures

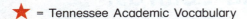
natural resource

Which **natural resource** is shown on the next page?

GLE 0207.7.3 Differentiate between renewable and non-renewable resources.

2 What Resources Do People Use?

A **natural resource** is something found in nature that people need or use.
Air, water, soil, and rocks are natural resources.
People use water for drinking, washing, and cooking.
They use soil to grow food.
Sometimes they use rocks to build their homes.

You use water to wash your hands.

A **renewable resource** is a natural resource that can be replaced by nature.

Water and wind are renewable resources.

Trees are renewable resources, too. Wood from trees is used to make houses and other things.

New trees are planted to replace the trees that are cut down.

Items from Trees

pencils

buildings

furniture

paper

1. How do people use water? Circle the words that answer this question.

2. List renewable resources.

_____

_____

_____

89

Circle the correct answer.

3. Which is a nonrenewable resource?

A water

B wind

C coal

GLE 0207.7.3

I Wonder . . . Earth has many resources. How can people save resources?

_____

_____

_____

90

Nonrenewable Resources

A **nonrenewable resource** is a natural resource that cannot be easily replaced once it has been used.

Coal and oil are nonrenewable resources.

Coal and oil are used to heat homes.

Saving Resources

Some nonrenewable resources cannot be replaced once they are used. Gas and oil cannot be replaced. People can save resources. They can ride a bike instead of drive a car.

Classify

What are three natural resources?

Summary

Renewable and nonrenewable resources are both found in nature.

Compare and contrast renewable and nonrenewable resources.

Renewable resource	Nonrenewable resource

 **Classify** What are three natural resources?

_____

_____

VOCABULARY

fossil Something that remains of a living thing from long ago. *(noun)*

imprint The shape of a living thing found in rock. *(noun)*

VOCABULARY ACTIVITY

Use Pictures

imprint

Look at the picture of the **imprint** on this page.

What makes an **imprint?**

_____

_____

GLE 0207.5.2 Draw conclusions from fossils about organisms that lived in the past.

3 What Are Fossils?

A **fossil** is something that remains of a living thing from long ago. Fossils form or are made in different ways.

How Casts Form

1 A living thing dies. It is covered by mud. The mud turns to rock.

2 The hard part of the living thing breaks down. Its imprint is left.

How Fossils Form

Some fossils are imprints.
An **imprint** is the shape of a living thing found in rock.
Some fossils are hard parts of animals, such as bones or teeth. These hard parts turn to rock after many, many years.

imprint

cast

3 Mud or minerals fill the imprint. A cast forms.

1. How is a cast different from an imprint?

_____

_____

2. What is the first step in forming a cast?

_____

3. (Circle) the imprints shown on these pages.

Circle the correct answer.

4. What can you learn from a dinosaur's tooth?

Ⓐ its size

Ⓑ what it ate

Ⓒ its weight

GLE 0207.5.2

I Wonder . . . Dinosaurs with sharp, pointed teeth ate meat. What kind of teeth would a dinosaur that ate plants have?

_____

_____

Learning from Fossils

Fossils tell us about plants and animals that lived long ago.
Fossil bones tell about the size of an animal.
Fossil teeth show if an animal ate plants or meat.

Skeleton of Tyrannosaurus rex

Sharp, pointed teeth show that the dinosaur ate meat.

The size of the leg bones show how tall the dinosaur was.

Imprints and casts show how a plant or an animal looked.
Tracks show how an animal moved from place to place.

Footprints tell about the weight of the dinosaur.

5. Look at the skeleton of the Tyrannosaurus rex on these pages. List what you know about this dinosaur.

_____

_____

6. What kind of teeth would a meat-eating dinosaur have? Draw the teeth.

Summary

Fossils form in different ways.

They give clues about plants and animals that lived long ago.

What can you learn by looking at the fish fossils?

_____

_____

 Compare and Contrast

What can different fossils tell us about animals?

Tyrannosaurus rex fossil	fish fossil

Clues to Earth's Past

Scientists study fossils to learn how places on Earth have changed over time.
A fish fossil is found on land.
Fish live in water.
Scientists can tell that a long time ago, the land was likely under water.

Compare And Contrast

What can different fossils tell us about animals?

K W L

What Did You Learn?

TCAP Practice

❶ Which is a renewable resource?

Ⓐ coal

Ⓑ oil

Ⓒ trees

GLE 0207.7.3

❷ Why is humus in soil important?

❸ What is a rock?

❹ Why do scientists study fossils?

K W L

What Did You Learn?

TCAP Practice

❶ Circle the letter of the correct answer.

❷ Humus is important because _____

_____.

❸ A rock is _____

_____.

❹ Scientists study fossils _____

_____.

Circle the correct answer.

1 Look at the picture.

Which layer has the most humus?

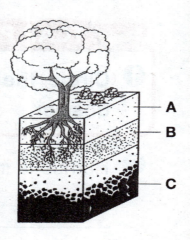

(A) layer A

(B) layer B

(C) layer C

 GLE 0207.7.1

2 Which is a renewable resource?

(A) oil

(B) iron ore

(C) water

 GLE 0207.7.3

3 Look at the picture.

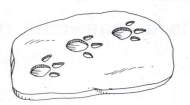

What can this fossil tell about the animal that made these tracks?

(A) what the animal looked like

(B) how much the animal weighed

(C) whether the animal ate meat or plants

 GLE 0207.5.2

4 **Minerals are**

(A) the same things as rocks

(B) found in rocks

(C) living things 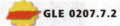 GLE 0207.7.2

5 **What kind of soil is best for growing vegetables?**

(A) soil with lots of humus

(B) soil with lots of clay

(C) soil with lots of sand 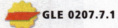 GLE 0207.7.1

6 **Which rock can be described as rough?**

(A)

(B)

(C)   GLE 0207.7.2

99

What Do You Know?

Talk with a partner.

Make a list of things that you can see in the sky.

_____

_____

_____

Visit www.eduplace.com/tnscp to learn more.

Motions in the Sky

Contents

What Do You Want to Know?

What do you wonder about the Sun and the planets?

_____

_____

VOCABULARY

planet A large object that moves around the Sun. (*noun*)

solar system The Sun and the space objects that move around it. (*noun*)

Sun The brightest object in the day sky. (*noun*)

VOCABULARY ACTIVITY

Use Words

Sun

What words on these two pages help you understand what the **Sun** is? Circle them.

GLE 0207.10.1 Explain why the sun is the primary source of the earth's energy.

1 What Makes Up the Solar System?

The **Sun** is the brightest thing in the day sky.
It is much larger than Earth.
The Sun looks small because it is very far away.

The Sun is made of hot gases.
The gases give off energy.
The Sun's energy comes to Earth
as light.
Some of the Sun's light is changed
to heat.

the Sun

1. Look at the picture of the girl. What tells you that the Sun is bright?

_____

_____

Circle the correct answer.

❷ What is the brightest thing in the day sky?

(A) Sun

(B) Earth

(C) Moon

GLE 0207.10.1

103

3. Fill in the blanks.

a. The Sun helps plants

_____ and _____.

b. The Sun's light helps

_____ and _____

see.

4. Some of the Sun's light is changed

to _____.

See page 220 for the Express Lab.

 0207.10.2

Living things on Earth use energy from the Sun.
The Sun helps plants live and grow.
The Sun's light helps people and animals to see.

The Sun warms the land.
It warms the air.
It warms water.
The Sun keeps people and animals warm, too.

5. List four things that the Sun warms.

_____

_____

_____

I Wonder . . . Living things on Earth need the Sun. What are some of the ways in which people use the Sun?

_____

_____

_____

6. The Sun and the space objects that move around it make up the

_____.

7. Look at the drawing on these two pages. The space objects moving around the Sun are called

_____.

The Solar System

The Sun and the space objects that move around it make up our **solar system**.
A **planet** is a large object that moves around the Sun.
Our solar system has many planets. Planets are always in the sky.

Jupiter

Saturn

Uranus

Neptune

Pluto
(dwarf planet)

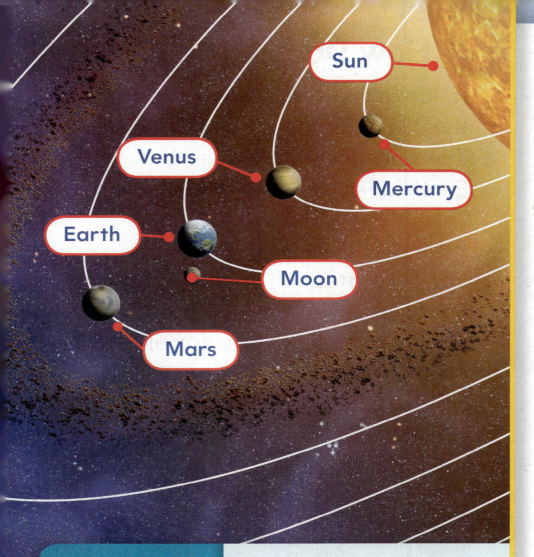

Sun

Venus

Mercury

Earth

Moon

Mars

Main Idea

What makes up the solar system?

Summary

The Sun, which gives us heat and light, is the center of the solar system. Circle the words on these pages that tell what makes up our solar system.

▶ **Main Idea** What makes up the solar system?

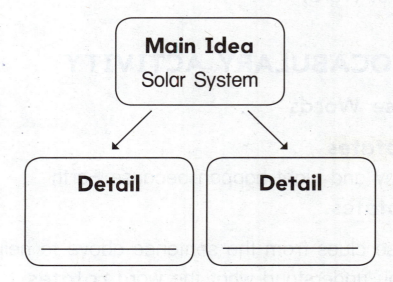

Main Idea
Solar System

Detail

Detail

VOCABULARY

orbit The path that one space object travels around another. *(noun)*

revolve To move in a path around an object. *(verb)*

rotates Spins around an imaginary line. *(verb)*

VOCABULARY ACTIVITY

Use Words

rotates

Day and night happen because Earth **rotates.**

Use clues from the sentence above to help you understand what the word **rotates** means.

GLE 0207.6.1 Realize that the sun is our nearest star and that its position in the sky appears to change.

2 How Does Earth Move?

It looks like the Sun moves across the sky each day.
The Sun does not move, but Earth does.

Earth Spins

Earth **rotates**, or spins around an imaginary line.
This make-believe line is called an axis.

Different parts of Earth face the Sun as Earth rotates.
It is day on the part of Earth that faces the Sun.
It is night on the part of Earth that faces away from the Sun.
It takes Earth one day to rotate one time.

axis

1. Put an X on the part of Earth where it is day.

2. How long does it take the Earth to rotate one time?

_____

3. List two ways in which shadows change.

a. _____

b. _____

4. Circle the shadows on these two pages.

Shadows Change

Light from the Sun shines on Earth.
Shadows are made when something
blocks the Sun's light.
Shadows change when Earth rotates.
Shadows change how long they are.
Shadows change where they are.

People can tell time by
looking at shadows.

Shadows Change

morning

The Sun is low
in the sky.
Shadows are long.
Shadows get shorter
and shorter until noon.

noon

The Sun is at its highest
point in the sky.
Shadows are shortest.

afternoon

The Sun is low in the
sky again.
Shadows grow longer.

TCAP Practice

Circle the correct answer.

❺ Shadows change because the Sun appears to move across the sky. When are shadows shortest?

Ⓐ morning

Ⓑ noon

Ⓒ afternoon

GLE 0207.6.1

6. Use your finger to trace the path of Earth around the Sun. What is this path called?

_____

7. Find winter in the picture. (Circle) the correct words.

a. Tennessee is tipped (toward / away from) the Sun.

b. Tennessee gets (more light / less light) in winter than in summer.

Earth Moves Around the Sun

Earth moves in another way as it rotates.
Earth and the other planets **revolve**, or move in a path, around the Sun. The path that one space object travels around another is called an **orbit**.

It takes one year for Earth to revolve around the Sun.

The seasons change as Earth orbits the Sun.
The part of Earth tipped toward the Sun gets the most light.
It is summer there.
The part of Earth tipped away from the Sun gets less light.
It is winter there.

Draw Conclusions

If it is spring, how long will it be until it is spring again?

Summary Earth moves in two different ways. It rotates and it revolves. What changes happen on Earth because the planet rotates?

_____

_____

_____

▶ **Draw Conclusions** If it is spring, how long will it be until it is spring again?

A year has four seasons:
spring, summer, fall, and winter.

_____

_____

VOCABULARY

Moon A large sphere made of rock. (*noun*)

phases The different ways the Moon looks. (*noun*)

VOCABULARY ACTIVITY

Use Words

Moon

Circle the words on this page that describe the **Moon.**

3 How Does the Moon Move?

The **Moon** is a large sphere made of rock.
It is the closest large space object to Earth.
It looks like the Moon moves across the sky at night.
This happens because Earth is rotating.

The Moon has mountains and craters, or pits. You can see dark spots on the Moon from Earth.

craters

The Moon in Motion

The Moon revolves in an orbit around Earth.
It takes about one month for the Moon to go around Earth one time. This happens month after month.

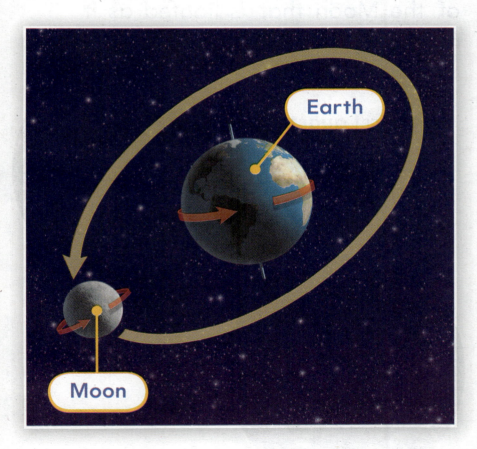

Earth

Moon

1. How does the Moon move?

_____

_____

2. Why does the Moon appear to move across the sky at night?

_____

_____

I Wonder . . . I know that the Moon does not always look the same. Why is the new Moon dark?

_____

_____

_____

The Changing Moon

The Moon does not have its own light.
It reflects the Sun's light.
The Sun shines on only one side of the Moon at a time.
You may only see part of the side of the Moon that is lighted as it revolves around Earth.

first quarter

new

The Moon looks a little different every night.
The different ways the Moon looks are called **phases**.

full

last quarter

Cause and Effect

Why does the Moon look bright in the night sky?

Summary The Moon is a large sphere of rock that orbits Earth. Draw and label the four phases of the Moon.

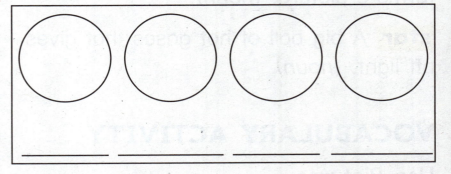

_____ _____ _____ _____

▶ **Cause and Effect** Why does the Moon look bright in the night sky?

Cause	Effect
_____ _____	The Moon looks bright.

117

VOCABULARY

constellation A group of stars that forms a picture. (*noun*)

star A big ball of hot gases that gives off light. (*noun*)

VOCABULARY ACTIVITY

Use Pictures

star

Say the word aloud.
Use clues from the pictures to help you understand what the word **star** means.

GLE 0207.6.1 Realize that the sun is our nearest star and that its position in the sky appears to change.

4 What Stars Can You See?

A **star** is a big ball of hot gases that gives off light.
Stars are always in the sky.
The Sun is the closest star to Earth.
The Sun's light is very bright.
You cannot see other stars during the day.

Stars are different colors.

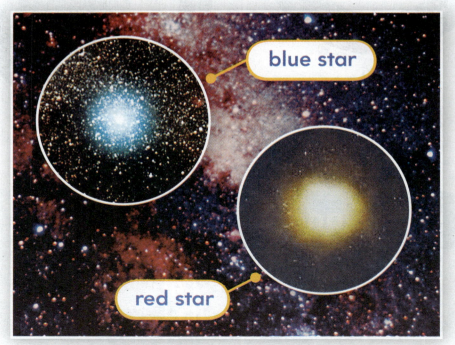

blue star

red star

You can see other stars at night when the sky is dark.
Other stars are very large, just like the Sun.
These stars look small because they are very far away.
Some stars look brighter than others.
Those stars may be bigger, hotter, or closer to Earth.

The Sun is a yellow star.

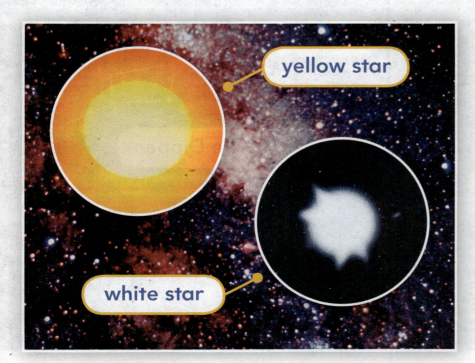

yellow star

white star

2. Stars are very large. Why do they look small in the night sky?

_____

_____

3. Underline the meaning of constellation on this page.

I Wonder . . . Could I make up my own constellations?

_____

_____

_____

Star Patterns

Some stars look like they make pictures.
A **constellation** is a group of stars that forms a picture.
Constellations have names.
Constellations can help you find some stars.

The star Polaris is in the Little Dipper.
Polaris is also called the North Star.

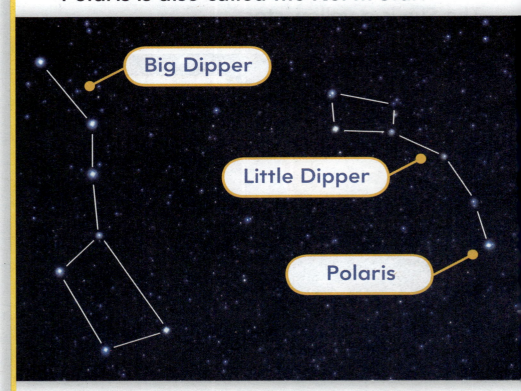

Big Dipper

Little Dipper

Polaris

Star Locations

It looks like stars move across the night sky.

This happens because Earth is spinning.

You see different parts of the night sky as Earth rotates.

The Little Dipper looks like it's moving because Earth is moving.

Compare and Contrast

How is the Sun different from other stars?

Summary

You can see stars in the night sky. Why do stars seem to move across the night sky?

_____

▶ **Compare and Contrast** How is the Sun different from other stars?

	Sun	Other Stars
How far away?	_____	_____
	_____	_____
When can it be seen?	_____	_____
	_____	_____

K W L
What Did You Learn?

TCAP Practice

❶ (Circle) the correct answer.

❷ _____ causes night and day on Earth.

❸ Some stars look brighter than others because _____

_____.

❹ The Sun helps living things

_____ and

_____.

Responding

K W L
What Did You Learn?

TCAP Practice

❶ **Stars in the night sky look smaller than our Sun because**

Ⓐ they are farther away from Earth.

Ⓑ they are closer to Earth than our Sun.

Ⓒ they can be seen during the day.

GLE 0207.6.1

❷ What causes night and day on Earth?

❸ Why do some stars look brighter than others?

❹ How does the Sun help living things?

Draw a picture to show how the Sun warms Earth.

Circle the correct answer.

1 **Look at the picture.**

What time of day is it?

(A) morning

(B) noon

(C) afternoon

 GLE 0207.6.1

2 **Earth gets heat, light, and energy from**

(A) the Moon

(B) the Sun

(C) the planets

 GLE 0207.10.1

3 **Look at the picture.**

What phase of the moon is it?

(A) new moon

(B) full moon

(C) last quarter

 GLE 0207.6.2

4 How long does it take Earth to rotate one time on its axis?

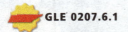 **A** a day

B a month

C a year

GLE 0207.6.1

5 The Sun is

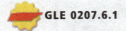 **A** a planet

B a constellation

C a star

GLE 0207.6.1

6 Look at this picture.

What will the ice cream look like in an hour?

A **B** **C**

GLE 0207.10.1

What Do You Know?

Talk with a partner.
Tell about the weather in the different seasons.

_____

_____

_____

Weather and Seasons

Visit www.eduplace.com/tnscp to learn more.

Contents

What Do You Want to Know?

What do you wonder about weather and seasons?

_____

_____

_____

_____

_____

VOCABULARY

season A time of year that has its own kind of weather. *(noun)*

spring The season that follows winter. *(noun)*

summer The season that follows spring. *(noun)*

VOCABULARY ACTIVITY

Classify Words

spring

Circle all the words on these pages that tell about spring.

1 What Is Weather Like in Spring and Summer?

A **season** is a time of year. It has its own kind of weather.

Spring

Spring is the season that follows winter. It is warmer in spring. Warmer weather and spring rain help plants grow.

Animals find food
when new plants grow.
Animals that were sleeping
in winter wake up.
Many baby animals are born
in spring.

I Wonder . . . Animals go
through many changes in spring.
I wonder what other changes happen
in spring.

_____

_____

TCAP Practice

Circle the correct answer.

1. **Which of the following words describe spring?**

   Ⓐ warmest season

   Ⓑ long hours of sunshine

   Ⓒ follows winter

GLE 0207.8.1

2. Tell about summer.

_____

_____

_____

3. What are some ways you try to stay cool in summer?

_____

_____

_____

Express Lab

See page 221 for the Express Lab.

Summer

Summer is the season that follows spring. Summer is the warmest season of the year. People try to stay cool. They wear clothing that keeps them cool.

Plants grow in summer.
Young animals grow, too.
Young animals learn to find food.
This lamb eats a growing plant.

Compare and Contrast

How are spring and summer different?

Summary

Spring and summer are times of warmth and new life. Tell about the weather in these seasons.

 ## Compare and Contrast

How are spring and summer different?

Spring	Summer

VOCABULARY

fall The season that follows summer. (*noun*)

winter The season that follows fall. (*noun*)

VOCABULARY ACTIVITY

Multiple-Meaning Words

fall

Look at this page. How is the word **fall** used on this page? What is another way you use the word **fall**?

_____

_____

_____

2 What Is Weather Like in Fall and Winter?

Fall is the season
that follows summer.
It is cooler in fall.
People wear warmer clothes.
Leaves drop from some trees.

Animals get ready
for colder weather.
Some animals grow thick fur.
Other animals move
to places that have more food.
Many animals store food
for winter.

I. What do animals do to get ready for
the cold weather?

_____

_____

_____

I Wonder . . . Some activities
change with seasons. Tell two activities
you do in fall and two you enjoy in winter.

_____

_____

_____

2. Circle words on these two pages that tell about winter.

Winter

Winter is the season
that follows fall.
It is the coldest season
of the year.
Snow falls in some places.

Sometimes it is hard for animals to find food.
Some plants die.
Many trees lose their leaves.

3. Draw what a tree looks like in cold winter weather.

4. Circle the sentence that tells what happens to animals in winter.

Circle the correct answer.

5. Which words describe plants in winter?

Ⓐ Plants grow.

Ⓑ Plants die.

Ⓒ Plants sprout.

GLE 0207.8.1

Summary

Fall and winter bring cooler weather and slower growth. Use your finger to trace arrows pointing to each season. Say each season as you touch the word. What shape did you trace?

 **Sequence**

What season comes before winter?

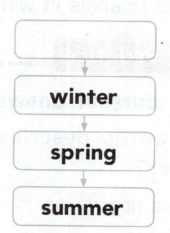

winter

spring

summer

The Pattern of Seasons

The seasons change in the same order every year.

The order is spring, summer, fall, and winter.

fall

summer

winter

spring

Sequence

What season comes before winter?

What Did You Learn?

❶ **Which season is the hottest?**

Ⓐ spring

Ⓑ fall

Ⓒ summer

GLE 0207.8.1

❷ What is a season?

❸ How is summer different than winter?

❹ Why do plants grow in spring?

What Did You Learn?

❶ ⟨Circle⟩ the correct answer.

❷ A season is _____

_____.

❸ Summer is _____

_____.

❹ Plants grow in spring because

_____.

Circle the correct answer.

1 Which of the following temperatures would **most likely** be measured in Tennessee during the summer?

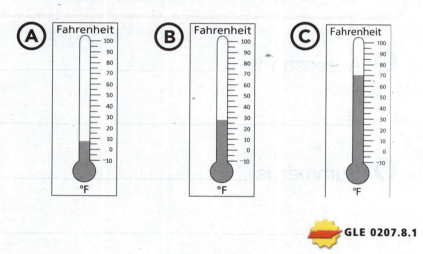

 GLE 0207.8.1

2 Many baby animals are born during the

Ⓐ spring

Ⓑ winter

Ⓒ fall

GLE 0207.8.1

3 Look at the chart.

| 88° | 84° | 80° | 86° |
| Monday | Tuesday | Wednesday | Thursday |

This chart **most likely** shows four days during which season?

Ⓐ winter

Ⓑ summer

Ⓒ fall

 GLE 0207.8.1

4 Which tool would you use to measure how much snow had fallen in the winter?

(A) a thermometer

(B) a ruler

(C) a balance

 GLE 0207.T/E.2

5 People are most likely to go swimming during

(A) fall

(B) winter

(C) summer

 GLE 0207.8.1

6 Look at the picture.

Which season comes after this season?

(A)

(B)

(C)

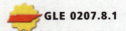 GLE 0207.8.1

What Do You Know?

Talk with a partner.

Draw an object.

Describe the object.

 Visit www.eduplace.com/tnscp to learn more.

Comparing Matter

Contents

What Do You Want to Know?

What do you want to know about matter?

_____

_____

How can you compare different objects?

_____

_____

VOCABULARY

gas A state of matter that spreads out to fill a space. *(noun)*

liquid A state of matter that does not have its own shape. *(noun)*

mass The amount of matter in an object. *(noun)*

★ **properties** Color, shape, size, odor, and texture. *(noun)*

solid A state of matter that has its own size and shape. *(noun)*

volume The amount of space a liquid takes up. *(noun)*

★ = Tennessee Academic Vocabulary

GLE 0207.9.1 Use tools to observe the physical properties of objects.
GLE 0207.9.3 Recognize that air takes up space.

1 How Can You Compare Matter?

You can tell about something by telling about its properties. Color, shape, size, odor, and texture are **properties**. Odor tells how something smells. Texture tells how something feels.

A balloon can be red or yellow.

A slipper can be soft and fuzzy.

A penny is round and flat.

You can tell about a thing by telling what materials were used to make it. For example, a penny is made of copper.

Marbles are made of glass.

These toy dinosaurs are made of plastic.

1. What are some properties that you can use to describe an object?

   a. _____

   b. _____

   c. _____

   d. _____

2. How are the penny and the marble alike and different?

Penny	Both	Marble
_____	_____	_____
_____	_____	_____
_____	_____	_____

3. Circle the object that light can pass through.

4. Label one object on this page with an A. Label another object on this page with a B.

a. List the properties of object A.

_____

_____

_____

b. List the properties of object B.

_____

_____

Other properties tell what something does.
Some things sink in water.
Other things float.
Some properties tell what the materials do.
Some things bend.
Other things break.
Some materials let light pass through.

This rock will sink in water.

A pencil will float in water.

Light can pass through these.

This toy can bend.

States of Matter

All things are made of matter.
The three states of matter are solid, liquid, and gas.
A **solid** is a state of matter that has its own size and shape.
A solid keeps its shape and size even if it is moved.

solid

A toy boat keeps its size and shape when you put it in water.

5. What are three states of matter?

a. _____

b. _____

c. _____

6. Put an X on something in the picture that is not a solid.

145

7. Underline the words that describe a liquid.

I Wonder . . . I know that water is a liquid. I know that a liquid does not have its own shape. What shape is the water in the pool?

_____

_____

A **liquid** is a state of matter that does not have its own shape. Liquids flow.
They take the shape of what holds them.

Juice takes the shape of the pitcher and glasses it is put in.

liquid

A **gas** is a state of matter that spreads out to fill a space.
A gas does not have its own shape.
It always fills a closed container.
The gas comes out when the container is opened.

A balloon holds a gas.

The beach ball holds a gas.

8. You cannot see the air inside a balloon. How do you know it is there?

_____

_____

9. Compare the gas in the beach ball with the liquid in the pool. How are they alike?

_____

_____

10. How do you measure the volume of a liquid?

_____

Circle the correct answer.

11. What would you use to measure how much space a solid takes up?

  Ⓐ a measuring cup

  Ⓑ a milk carton

  Ⓒ a ruler

GLE 0207.9.1

Using Tools to Measure

All matter takes up space. You can measure how much space matter takes up. You can use a ruler to measure how long a solid is. You can use a ruler to measure how wide or how high a solid is, too. You can use a measuring cup to measure the amount of space that a liquid takes up, or **volume**.

You pour a liquid into a measuring cup to find its volume.

All matter has mass.
Mass is the amount of matter in an object.
You can use a balance to measure the mass of something.

Classify

Name two properties that can be measured.

Put the object you want to measure on one side of the balance.

Add mass units until the sides are even.

balance

Summary

You can describe objects by their properties. How do tools help you describe an object's properties?

_____

_____

▶ **Classify**   Name two properties that can be measured.

Properties You Can Measure		
Ruler	Measuring Cup	Balance

VOCABULARY

 dissolves Mixes completely with water. *(verb)*

mixture Something made of two or more things. *(noun)*

separate To take apart. *(verb)*

★ = Tennessee Academic Vocabulary

VOCABULARY ACTIVITY

Use Syllables

separate

Break the word into syllables.

Say each syllable aloud.

Clap once for each syllable.

How many syllables does this word have?

GLE 0207.9.2 Investigate how temperature changes affect the state of matter.

2 How Does Matter Change?

A **mixture** is something made of two or more things.
You can put matter together to make a mixture.
There is no new matter in a mixture.

Trail mix is a mixture.
It is easy to separate.

You can take apart, or **separate**, a mixture.
Each part is still there.
Some mixtures are easy to separate.
The parts stay the same.
The parts are easy to see.

Trail Mix
2 cups cereal
1 cup raisins
1 cup peanuts
1 cup dry fruit

1. (Circle) the mixture on these pages. Put an X on the parts that make up the mixture.

2. List the parts that make up the trail mix.

a. _____

b. _____

c. _____

d. _____

I Wonder . . . What other mixture is hard to separate?

_____

_____

_____

3. Circle the word that makes the sentence true.

When you stir drink mix powder into water, the powder (separates, dissolves) in the water.

Some mixtures are hard to separate. When you stir drink mix powder with water, it **dissolves**, or mixes completely with the water.

152

The powder breaks into small bits that are too small to see. But it is still powder.

The drink mix powder dissolves in the water.

4. Tell whether each mixture would be hard or easy to separate.

Mixture	Hard or Easy
salad	_____
glue	_____
collection of seashells	_____
hot chocolate	_____

5. Look at the pictures on these two pages. List three ways to change solid matter.

a. _____

b. _____

c. _____

6. How can you change a sheet of paper?

_____

_____

Changing Matter

You can change solid matter in many ways.

You can cut matter to change its shape.

You can break matter into smaller pieces to change its size or shape.

cutting paper

You can pound clay to make it flat.
You can sand wood to make it smooth.
These kinds of changes do not change the material that the matter is made of.

pounding clay

sanding wood

7. Cutting, sanding, and pounding can change the shape of _____.

8. Some liquids change to _____ when you take away heat.

TCAP Practice

(Circle) the correct answer.

9. **Some solids will change to liquids when**

Ⓐ heat is added

Ⓑ heat is taken away

Ⓒ they are mixed with other solids

GLE 0207.9.2

Express Lab

See page 222 for the Express Lab.

 0207.9.2

156

Changing States

Matter can change from one state to another.
Some liquids can change to solids when you take away heat.
Other solids can change to liquids when you add heat.

**The juice in the pitcher is a liquid.
The juice in the tray is a solid.
The juice on the plate is changing from a solid to a liquid.**

All matter does not change the same way when you heat it. Some things melt fast. Some things melt slowly. Other things do not melt at all.

Draw Conclusions

If a solid changes to a liquid, what can you say happened?

Butter melts fast.

Summary

Matter can be changed in many different ways. If you add a small amount of heat to ice and to a plastic toy, which item would melt faster?

_____

▶ **Draw Conclusions** If a solid changes to a liquid, what can you say happened?

> **Fact:** Matter can change from one state to another.

> **Fact:** Some solids can change to _____ when you add _____.

> **Conclusion:** _____

VOCABULARY

★ **magnify** To make objects look larger. *(verb)*

★ = Tennessee Academic Vocabulary

VOCABULARY ACTIVITY

Use Words

In the picture on this page, the children

are using a _____ to magnify the small parts of matter.

3 How Does Matter Look Up Close?

Matter is made of very small parts. The parts are too little to see with only your eyes.
You can use a tool to see these small parts.

The children are using a hand lens.

hand lens

GLE 0207.9.1 Use tools to observe the physical properties of objects.

Tools that Magnify

Some tools can make objects look larger, or **magnify** them.
A hand lens can make objects look bigger.
A microscope can magnify objects even more.

Scientists use microscopes to magnify objects.

microscope

1. Circle the hand lens.
2. Circle the microscope.
3. What do these tools do?

_____

_____

Circle the correct answer.

4. Compared to a hand lens, an ant magnified under the microscope looks

Ⓐ bigger

Ⓑ smaller

Ⓒ the same size

GLE 0207.9.1

5. Draw lines. Match each object to what it might look like when magnified.

flower

clothing

insect

160

Ants Up Close

Ants look like this without a magnifying tool.

An ant looks like this through a hand lens.

An ant looks like this through a microscope.

Matter Up Close

You can see the small parts of matter when you use a tool to magnify an object.

feather

fish scales

sugar cube

strawberry

Main Idea and Details

Why are tools needed to see small parts of matter?

Summary

Matter is made of parts too small to see with only your eyes.
What might you learn by magnifying a grasshopper?

▶ **Main Idea**   Why are tools needed to see small parts of matter?

Main Idea
Tools help you see small parts of matter.

Detail
Some tools make objects look

_____.

Detail
Some tools help you see

_____.

VOCABULARY

gravity A force that pulls all objects toward each other. *(noun)*

⭐ **weight** A measure of the pull of gravity on an object. *(noun)*

⭐ = Tennessee Academic Vocabulary

VOCABULARY ACTIVITY

Use Pictures

gravity

Say the word aloud.
Use clues from the picture to help you understand what **gravity** means.

GLE 0207.12.2 Realize that things fall toward the ground unless something holds them up.

---

4 What Makes Things Fall?

Drop a ball.
Gravity will make it fall to the ground.
Gravity is a force that pulls all objects toward each other.
It makes objects near Earth fall to the ground.

Gravity makes water move down.

Gravity pulls on
the glass and
the juice in it.
The table keeps
it from falling.
Push the glass
off the table.
The glass and juice
fall toward Earth.

Circle the correct answer.

1. What caused the objects to fall
to the ground?

Ⓐ water

Ⓑ air

Ⓒ gravity

GLE 0207.12.2

I Wonder . . . What would
happen to the glass if there were no
gravity?

_____

_____

_____

2. Underline the definition of weight.

3. What is mass?

_____

_____

_____

4. Circle the object that has more mass. Tell how you know.

_____

_____

_____

Gravity and Weight

Weight is how much gravity pulls on an object.

The pull of gravity is stronger on objects that have more mass.

Mass is how much material is in an object.

The toy elephant has more mass.
Gravity pulls on it more.
It is heavier.

A big rock has a
lot of mass.
The pull of gravity
on the rock is strong.
It weighs a lot.
A feather has
little mass.
The pull of gravity
is not as strong.
It weighs less.

The rock is heavier than the feather.

Summary

The pull of gravity is stronger on objects that have more mass.
Will the pull of gravity be stronger on a book or a pen?

▶ **Draw Conclusions**

How can you tell that one object is heavier than another?

Fact
The pull of gravity is stronger on objects that are heavier.

↓

Conclusion

Draw Conclusions

How can you tell that one object is heavier than another?

KWL

What Did You Learn?

TCAP Practice

❶ Circle the correct answer.

❷ A _____ and a _____ can help you see small parts of things.

❸ Gravity is

_____

_____

❹ Some mixtures are harder to separate than others because

_____

_____

KWL

What Did You Learn?

TCAP Practice

❶ A _____ spreads out to fill a closed container.

Ⓐ gas

Ⓑ liquid

Ⓒ solid

GLE 0207.9.3

❷ What two tools can help you see small parts of things?

❸ What is gravity?

❹ Why are some mixtures harder to separate than others?

Draw a picture to show how matter can change.

Circle the correct answer.

1 **Gravity is a force that makes things**

   (A) melt when it is hot

   (B) fall to the ground

   (C) float in water

 GLE 0207.12.2

2 **Which tool can you use to measure volume?**

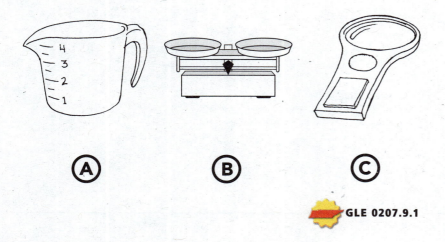

   (A)   (B)   (C)

GLE 0207.9.1

3 **What is an example of a liquid becoming a solid?**

   (A) water boiling

   (B) water freezing into ice

   (C) ice melting into water

 GLE 0207.9.2

4 **Look at the picture.**

What will happen if you let air out of this balloon?

(A) The balloon will not change.

(B) The balloon will get rounder.

(C) The balloon will get flatter.

 GLE 0207.9.3

5 **Which weighs the most?**

(A) an object with a lot of mass

(B) an object with very little mass

(C) an object with no mass  GLE 0207.9.1

6 **Look at the picture.**

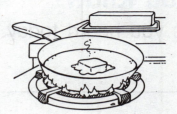

Why is the butter melting?

(A) It has more space to fill.

(B) It is touching metal.

(C) Heat has been added to it.

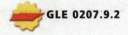 GLE 0207.9.2

169

KWL

What Do You Know?

List the sounds you heard today.

_____

_____

_____

Pick one sound from your list.
Describe what you heard.

_____

_____

Go Digital → Visit www.eduplace.com/tnscp to learn more.

Making Sound

Contents

What Do You Want to Know?

What do you wonder about sounds?

_____

_____

_____

_____

_____

_____

_____

_____

_____

_____

_____

VOCABULARY

energy The ability to cause change. *(noun)*

★ **sound** A form of energy that you hear. *(noun)*

sound waves The waves that move vibrating air. *(noun)*

★ **vibrate** When an object moves back and forth very quickly. *(verb)*

★ = Tennessee Academic Vocabulary

VOCABULARY ACTIVITY

Use Words

vibrate

Pluck the strings to make them **vibrate.** Use clues from the sentence to know what **vibrate** means.

GLE 0207.11.1 Investigate how vibrating objects produce sound.

1 How Is Sound Made?

Energy is the ability to change things.

Sound is energy that you hear. Sound is made when an object vibrates.

Vibrate means to move back and forth very fast.

The boy makes sound.

This is a banjo.
It has strings.
You pull on the strings to
make sound.
That makes the strings vibrate.
It makes the air vibrate, too.
You cannot see air vibrate.
You can hear it as sound.

**The girl makes
sound, too.**

strings

Circle the correct answer.

1. **Energy that you hear is**

Ⓐ light

Ⓑ sound

Ⓒ heat

GLE 0207.11.1

I Wonder . . . Instruments can
vibrate to create sounds. Name the
parts of instruments that vibrate.

_____

_____

See page 223 for the Express Lab.

 0207.11.1

173

2. (Circle) the parts of the alarm clock that vibrate to make sound.

3. Tell how you hear the sound of the alarm clock.

_____

_____

_____

How You Hear

You use your ears to hear sound.
Air vibrates.
It moves in waves called
sound waves.
Sound waves move into your ear.
You hear a sound.

ear

This is a hearing aid.
Some people use it to help them hear.
They put the hearing aid in their ear.
It helps them hear sound.

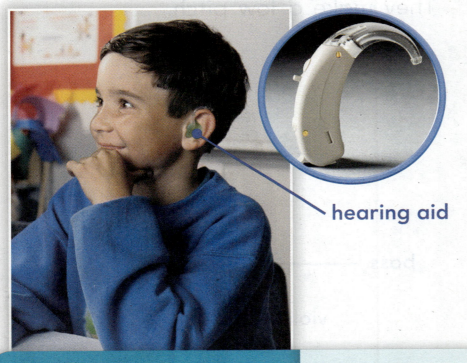

hearing aid

Summary

Sound is made when an object vibrates.
Sound waves move into your ear.
What sounds do you hear right now?

_____

_____

Cause and Effect

What causes a person to hear sounds?

Cause	Effect
	A person hears sounds.

Cause and Effect

What causes a person to hear sounds?

175

VOCABULARY

pitch How high or low a sound is. *(noun)*

VOCABULARY ACTIVITY

Find All the Meanings

pitch

A word can have more than one meaning.
You may know that **pitch** means to throw a ball.
The word **pitch** also means how high or low a sound is.

GLE 0207.11.1 Investigate how vibrating objects produce sound.
GLE 0207.11.2 Classify sounds according to their loudness and pitch.

2 What Is Pitch?

You can tell about sound by its pitch.
Pitch is how high or low a sound is.
Some things vibrate fast.
They make a high pitch.
Some things do not vibrate fast.
They make a low pitch.

bass

violin

The violin strings vibrate fast. It has a higher pitch than the bass.

Short things make a high pitch.
Long things make a low pitch.

A short straw makes a high pitch.

I. Look at the picture on this page.

a. (Circle) the straw on the instrument with the lowest pitch.

b. Tell why it has the lowest pitch.

_____

_____

2. Look at the instruments on these pages. What vibrates to make sound?

_____

_____

I Wonder . . . I know that a flute has a lower pitch than a piccolo. What instrument has a pitch that is lower than a flute?

_____

TCAP Practice

Circle the correct answer.

3. Which animal makes a sound with the highest pitch?

   (A) horse

   (B) cow

   (C) mouse

GLE 0207.11.2

Comparing Pitch

low pitch	high pitch
flute	piccolo
cow	canary
school bell	jingle bells

Changing Pitch

You can change the pitch of a sound.
Play a guitar.
You can make the pitch high by holding down the strings.
This makes the strings short.
Short strings have a high pitch.

Long strings have a low pitch.

4. (Circle) the part of the instrument that vibrates to make the sound.

5. (Circle) the guitar below that is making the lower pitch.
How do you know?

_____

6. On what other string instruments can the pitch be changed?

_____

Summary

Pitch is how high or low a sound is.
You can change the pitch of a sound.
How can the boy change the pitch of
the whistle?

_____

_____

▶ **Main Idea** How can you change
the pitch of an instrument?

Main Idea

The pitch of an instrument
can change.

180

Sound is made in some objects.
Change how long the object is.
The pitch will change, too.

The boy changes how
long the whistle is.

Main Idea

How can you change the pitch of
an instrument?

What Is a Sound's Volume?

Volume is how loud or soft a sound is.
Sound waves can be big or small.
Big sound waves have a lot of energy.
They make loud sounds.
Small sound waves have little energy.
They make soft sounds.

A whisper is a soft sound.

VOCABULARY

volume How loud or soft a sound is. (*noun*)

VOCABULARY ACTIVITY

Use Syllables

volume

Break the word into syllables.
Say each syllable aloud.
Clap once for each syllable.
How many syllables does **volume** have?

_____

 GLE 0207.11.1 Investigate how vibrating objects produce sound.
GLE 0207.11.2 Classify sounds according to their loudness and pitch.

181

I. What are two things that affect how loud or soft a sound is to the person who hears it?

a. _____

_____

b. _____

_____

I Wonder . . . Sounds have different volumes. What makes a siren louder than a whisper?

_____

_____

_____

A sound can seem to get loud as you get close to it.
It seems to get soft as you move away.

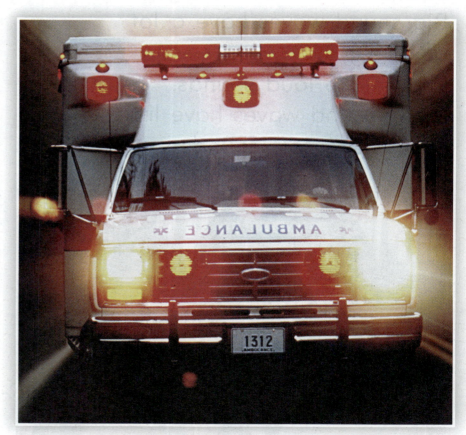

A loud siren alerts you to danger.

Comparing Pitch and Volume

You know that pitch is how high or low a sound is.

Volume is how loud or soft a sound is.

Sounds with low pitches can have a loud or soft volume.

A boat horn has a loud volume. A heartbeat has a low volume. They both have a low pitch.

heartbeat

boat horn

TCAP Practice

Circle the correct answer.

2. **Which makes a sound with a high pitch and a loud volume?**

    (A) a bear

    (B) a boat horn

    (C) a smoke alarm

GLE 0207.11.2

3. Circle the animal that makes a sound with the lower pitch.

183

Summary

Volume is how loud or soft a sound is. Sounds can have a high or low pitch. Sounds can have a loud or soft volume. Describe a sound that you hear on the playground.

_____

_____

 Compare and Contrast

How can two sounds be alike and different?

Compare	Contrast

184

Sounds with high pitches can have a loud or soft volume, too.

mouse

whistle

A mouse has a soft volume. A whistle has a loud volume. They both have a high pitch.

Compare and Contrast

How can two sounds be alike and different?

KWL

What Did You Learn?

TCAP Practice

❶ _____ is how loud or soft a sound is.

Ⓐ Energy

Ⓑ Pitch

Ⓒ Volume

GLE 0207.11.2

❷ How is sound made?

❸ What kind of sound is made by fast vibrations?

❹ You have tall and short empty bottles. Describe the sounds that the bottles make.

KWL

What Did You Learn?

TCAP Practice

❶ (Circle) the correct answer.

❷ Sound is made _____

_____.

❸ _____ are made by fast vibrations.

❹ The taller bottle will make _____

_____.

The shorter bottle will make _____

_____.

Circle the correct answer.

1 Look at the picture.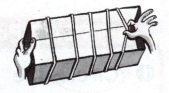

Why will letting go of the rubber band make sound?

(A) It will make the rubber band hot.

(B) It will put more air in the box.

(C) The rubber band will vibrate.

 GLE 0207.11.1

2 A sound wave with a lot of energy makes a sound that

(A) is loud

(B) is soft

(C) has a high pitch

 GLE 0207.11.2

3 Look at the picture.

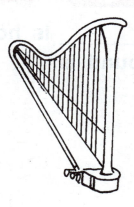

Which strings on this harp have the highest pitch?

(A) the shorter ones

(B) the longer ones

(C) the ones in the middle    GLE 0207.11.2

186

4 What is the <u>best</u> description of a sound wave?

(A) water moving

(B) air vibrating

(C) a breeze blowing

GLE 0207.11.1

5 How does a hearing aid help a person who can't hear soft sounds?

(A) It increases the pitch of sounds.

(B) It increases the volume of sounds.

(C) It increases the vibrations of sounds.

GLE 0207.T/E.2

6 Which animal makes a sound with the loudest volume?

(A)

(B)

(C)

GLE 0207.11.2

What Do You Know?

Talk with a partner.

Describe magnets that you have seen.

Make a list of things you know about magnets.

_____

_____

_____

_____

_____

_____

_____

Go Digital ✖ Visit www.eduplace.com/tnscp to learn more.

Magnets

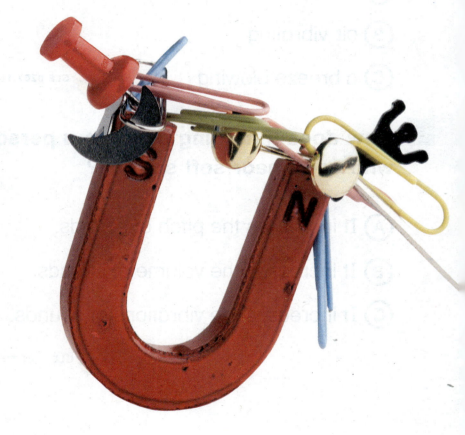

Contents

What Do You Want to Know?

What do you wonder about magnets?

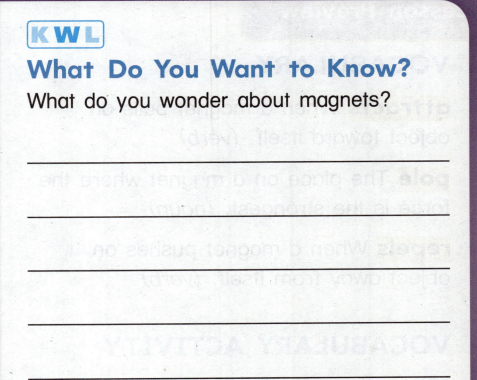

_____

_____

_____

_____

VOCABULARY

attracts When a magnet pulls an object toward itself. *(verb)*

pole The place on a magnet where the force is the strongest. *(noun)*

repels When a magnet pushes an object away from itself. *(verb)*

VOCABULARY ACTIVITY

Use Pictures

pole

The **poles** of a magnet can be marked with N or S.
Look at the picture of the magnets on this page.
Where are the **poles**?

GLE 0207.12.1 Experiment with magnets to determine that objects can move without being touched.

1 What Can Magnets Do?

Magnets come in many shapes and sizes.
Some magnets are flat and straight.
Others are curved or round.
All magnets can push or pull some things.
Pushes and pulls are forces.

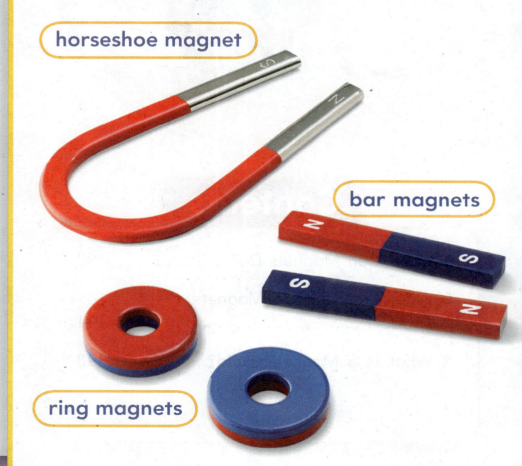

horseshoe magnet

bar magnets

ring magnets

Magnets Have Poles

All magnets have two poles.
A **pole** is the place on a
magnet where the force is
the strongest.
The poles are in different
places on different magnets.
The N on a magnet stands
for north pole.
The S stands for south pole.

1. Circle the poles on the magnets
   shown on these pages.

I Wonder . . . All magnets have
two poles. How can I find the poles on
a ring magnet?

_____

_____

_____

2. Which pole of a magnet would be attracted by a north pole of another magnet?

_____

TCAP Practice

⊙Circle the correct answer.

3. **What happens when unlike poles of two magnets are next to each other?**

   Ⓐ They attract each other.

   Ⓑ They repel each other.

   Ⓒ They do not move.

GLE 0207.12.1

See page 224 for the Express Lab.

 0207.12.1

Magnets Act on Each Other

All magnets push or pull other magnets.

Try putting the north pole of a magnet near the south pole of another magnet.

The magnets attract.

When a magnet **attracts**, it pulls something toward itself.

Unlike poles attract each other.

Unlike poles attract, or pull toward each other.

Try putting two north poles near each other.
The magnets repel.
When a magnet **repels**, it pushes something away from itself.
The same thing happens when you put two south poles together.

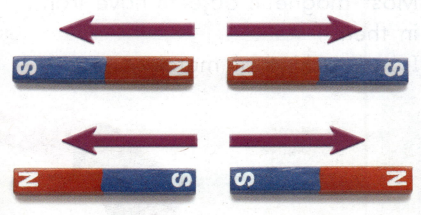

Like poles repel, or push away from each other.

Cause and Effect

What happens when like poles are near each other?

Summary
Magnets can push or pull things.
All magnets have two poles.
Where is the force strongest on magnets?

 ### Cause and Effect

What happens when like poles are near each other?

Cause	Effect
Like poles are near each other.	

VOCABULARY

magnetic Attracted by a magnet. (*adjective*)

nonmagnetic Not attracted by a magnet. (*adjective*)

VOCABULARY ACTIVITY

Use Pictures

magnetic

Look at the picture of the **magnetic** objects on this page.

What do you know about **magnetic** objects from this picture?

_____

GLE 0207.12.1 Experiment with magnets to determine that objects can move without being touched.

2 What Materials Do Magnets Attract?

Magnets can attract other magnets. Magnets can attract other things, too.

Magnetic Objects

Something is **magnetic** if it is attracted by a magnet. Most magnetic objects have iron in them. Iron is a kind of metal.

These objects are magnetic.

Nonmagnetic Objects

Some things are not attracted by magnets.
Something is **nonmagnetic** if it is not attracted by a magnet.
Glass is nonmagnetic.
Paper is nonmagnetic.
Wood is nonmagnetic.
Plastic is nonmagnetic, too.

These objects are nonmagnetic.

1. How can you tell if an object is magnetic?

_____

_____

_____

I Wonder . . . Magnets are in things we use every day. Which things in my home have magnets in them?

_____

_____

_____

Everyday Magnets

Many things use magnetic force to help them work.

Computer games have magnets in them.

Magnets help keep refrigerator doors closed.

Some toy cars have magnets in them.

The magnets make their motors run.

A can opener cuts the lid of a can.
A magnet lifts the lid off the can.

Have you ever used a compass?
Ships at sea use a compass.
A compass has a magnet in it.
A compass helps you find direction.
The compass needle always
points north.

compass needle

Compare and Contrast

How are magnetic and nonmagnetic objects different?

Summary

All magnets have forces that act on other magnets. Objects that are attracted by magnets are magnetic. Draw and label an object that is magnetic.

▶ Compare and Contrast

How are magnetic and nonmagnetic objects different?

Magnetic	Nonmagnetic

VOCABULARY

magnetic field The area around a magnet where the magnet's force works. *(noun)*

VOCABULARY ACTIVITY

Use Pictures

magnetic field

Look at the picture of the **magnetic field** on the next page.

What do you know about a **magnetic field** from the picture?

_____

_____

GLE 0207.12.1 Experiment with magnets to determine that objects can move without being touched.

3 What Is a Magnetic Field?

A magnet's force is different around different parts of the magnet. The force is strongest near the poles of the magnet. The force is less strong away from the poles.

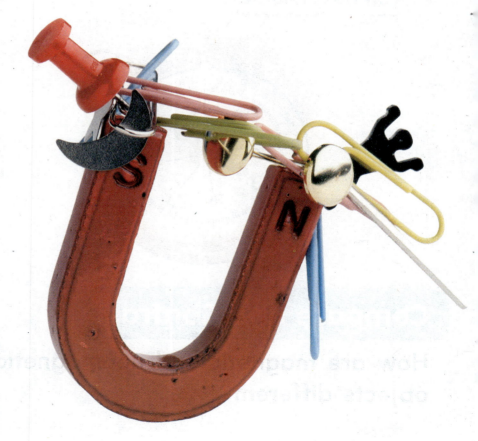

A magnet has a magnetic field.
A **magnetic field** is the area around
a magnet where the magnet's
force works.
A magnet works only when
something is in its magnetic field.

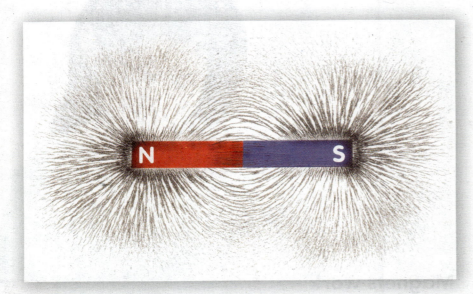

The iron filings show the magnetic field of
this magnet. You can see that the field is
strongest at the poles.

1. When does a magnet work?

_____

_____

2. (Circle) where the magnetic field is
   strongest on the magnet shown here.

3. How do you know that a magnet's force works through water and glass?

_____

_____

_____

Magnets Work Through Materials

A magnet can move things without touching them.
A magnet's force works through paper, glass, and water.
It works through air, too.

Magnets work through glass and water.

A magnet's force can also work through plastic.
Try putting plastic over a magnetic object.
Move the magnet over the plastic.
The magnetic object will still move toward the magnet.

Magnets work through plastic.

I Wonder . . . Magnets work through the toy's plastic. What is under the plastic that is attracted to the magnet?

_____

_____

TCAP Practice

Circle the correct answer.

4. What will happen to a paper clip on your desk if you hold a magnet under the desktop?

Ⓐ The magnet will attract the paper clip.

Ⓑ The magnet will not attract the paper clip.

Ⓒ The magnet will repel the paper clip.

GLE 0207.12.1

Summary

A magnet works only when something is in its magnetic field. What will happen when plastic is placed within the magnetic field of a magnet? Tell why.

_____

_____

 Main Idea

What are three materials that magnets can work through?

```
        ( Magnets can
          work through )
              |
    ┌─────────┼─────────┐
  (     )   (     )   (     )
```

Weakening a Magnet's Force

A magnet's force can attract many pins through one piece of paper.
Add more pieces of paper.
What happens?
The magnet attracts fewer pins.
The pins are farther away from the magnetic field.
The magnet's force is not as strong.

Main Idea

What are three materials that magnets can work through?

What Did You Learn?

TCAP Practice

❶ **What is the place on a magnet where the force is strongest?**

Ⓐ pole

Ⓑ magnetic field

Ⓒ force

GLE 0207.12.1

❷ What happens when you put the north pole of one magnet near the south pole of another magnet?

❸ What is something that is nonmagnetic?

❹ Tell why a magnet can hold a thin photograph to a refrigerator door but cannot hold a thick picture frame to the door.

K W L

What Did You Learn?

TCAP Practice

❶ Circle the correct answer.

❷ The magnets _____ each other.

❸ _____ is nonmagnetic.

❹ A magnet cannot hold a thick picture frame to a refrigerator door because

_____.

Circle the correct answer.

1 **Which is magnetic?**

Ⓐ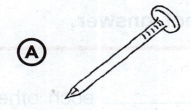

Ⓑ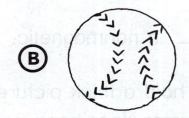

Ⓒ

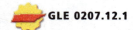 GLE 0207.12.1

2 **What is a pole on a magnet?**

Ⓐ the top of the magnet

Ⓑ the place where a magnet's force is strongest

Ⓒ the place where a magnet's force is weakest

GLE 0207.12.1

3 **A magnet is put near a book. What will happen?**

Ⓐ The magnet will move toward the book.

Ⓑ The book will move toward the magnet.

Ⓒ The book and the magnet will not move on their own. GLE 0207.12.1

4 **Look at the picture.**

The two magnets will

Ⓐ attract each other

Ⓑ repel each other

Ⓒ not attract or repel each other

 GLE 0207.12.1

5 **In which direction does a compass needle point?**

Ⓐ east

Ⓑ west

Ⓒ north

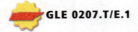 GLE 0207.T/E.1

6 **Look at the picture.**

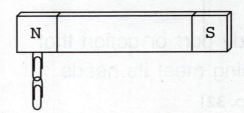

What would happen if you put a piece of paper between the magnet and the paper clips?

Ⓐ The paper clips would no longer be attracted to the magnet.

Ⓑ The paper clips would still be attracted to the magnet.

Ⓒ The paper clips would fall down.

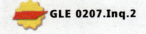 GLE 0207.Inq.2

Glossary

Ⓐ

adaptation A body part or action that helps a living thing meet its needs where it lives. **(p. 32)**

attracts When a magnet pulls an object toward itself. **(p. 192)**

Ⓒ

cone A part of a nonflowering plant where seeds form. **(p. 19)**

constellation A group of stars that forms a picture. **(p. 120)**

Ⓓ

★ **dissolves** Mixes completely with water. **(p. 152)**

Ⓔ

energy The ability to cause change. **(pp. 70, 172)**

environment All of the living and nonliving things around a living thing. **(p. 54)**

Glossary

F

fall The season that follows summer. (p. 132)

fibrous root A root that has many thin branches. (p. 23)

flower The plant part where fruit and seeds form. (p. 14)

food chain The order in which energy passes from one living thing to another. (p. 73)

food web A model that shows how different food chains are related. (p. 76)

fossil Something that remains of a living thing from long ago. (p. 92)

fruit The part of a flower that grows around a seed. (p. 14)

G

gas A state of matter that spreads out to fill a space. (p. 147)

gravity A force that pulls all objects toward each other. (p. 162)

 = Tennessee Academic Vocabulary

Glossary

★ **habitat** The part of an environment where a plant or an animal lives. **(p. 58)**

humus Tiny bits of dead plants and animals in soil. **(p. 86)**

imprint The shape of a living thing found in rock. **(p. 93)**

larva The wormlike stage in an insect's life cycle. **(p. 44)**

life cycle The series of changes that a living thing goes through as it grows. **(p. 24)**

liquid A state of matter that does not have its own shape. **(p.146)**

living thing Something that grows and changes. **(p. 6)**

Glossary

Ⓜ

magnetic Attracted by a magnet. **(p. 194)**

magnetic field The area around a magnet where the magnet's force acts. **(p. 199)**

⭐ **magnify** To make objects look larger. **(p. 159)**

mass The amount of matter in an object. **(p. 149)**

mineral A nonliving solid found in nature. **(p. 84)**

mixture Something made of two or more things. **(p. 150)**

Moon A large sphere made of rock. **(p. 114)**

Ⓝ

⭐ **natural resource** Something found in nature that people need or use. **(p. 88)**

⭐ = Tennessee Academic Vocabulary

209

Glossary

nonmagnetic Not attracted by a magnet. **(p. 195)**

nonrenewable resource A natural resource that cannot easily be replaced once it has been used. **(p. 90)**

nutrient A material in soil that helps a plant live and grow. **(p. 13)**

★ **offspring** The group of living things that come from the same living thing. **(p. 36)**

orbit The path that one space object travels around another. **(p. 112)**

phases The different ways the Moon looks. **(p. 117)**

pitch How high or low a sound is. **(p. 176)**

Glossary

planet A large object that moves around the Sun. **(p. 106)**

★ **properties** Color, shape, size, odor, and texture. **(p. 142)**

pole The place on a magnet where the force is the strongest. **(p. 191)**

pupa The stage between larva and adult when an insect changes form. **(p. 45)**

Ⓡ

renewable resource A natural resource that can be replaced by nature. **(p. 89)**

repels When a magnet pushes an object away from itself. **(p. 193)**

reproduce To make more living things of the same kind. **(p. 35)**

resource Something that plants and animals use to live. **(p. 68)**

★ = Tennessee Academic Vocabulary

Glossary

revolve To move in a path around an object. **(p. 112)**

rock A solid made of one or more minerals. **(p. 85)**

rotates Spins around an imaginary line. **(p. 108)**

S

season A time of year that has its own kind of weather. **(p. 128)**

seed The part from which a new plant grows. **(p. 14)**

seedling A young plant that grows from a seed. **(p. 24)**

separate To take apart. **(p. 151)**

Glossary

shelter A place where a living thing can be safe. **(p. 8)**

soil The loose material that covers Earth's surface. **(p. 86)**

solar system The Sun and the space objects that move around it. **(p. 106)**

solid A state of matter that has its own size and shape. **(p. 145)**

⭐ **sound** A form of energy that you hear. **(p. 172)**

sound waves The waves that move vibrating air. **(p. 174)**

spring The season that follows winter. **(p. 128)**

star A big ball of hot gases that gives off light. **(p. 118)**

stream A small river. **(p. 62)**

 = Tennessee Academic Vocabulary

213

Glossary

summer The season that follows spring. **(p. 130)**

Sun The brightest object in the day sky. **(p. 102)**

T

taproot A root that has one main branch. **(p. 22)**

V

★ **vibrate** When an object moves back and forth very fast. **(p. 172)**

volume **1.** The amount of space a liquid takes up. **(p. 148)**

2. How loud or soft a sound is. **(p. 181)**

Glossary

weight A measure of the pull of gravity on an object. **(p. 164)**

winter The season that follows fall. **(p. 134)**

woodland A place with many trees and bushes. **(p. 66)**

 = Tennessee Academic Vocabulary

Go Digital Visit www.eduplace.com/tnscp to learn more.

Investigate Shelters

⏱ **in 10 minutes**
Materials: paper, pencil, shelter pictures

1. Look at the pictures. Choose an animal shelter.
2. Think about which animals might use the shelter.
3. Make a list of the animals you might see.

Use with page 9.

 0207.2.1

Describe a Habitat

🕐 **in 5 minutes**

Materials: paper, pencil

1. Think of an animal.
2. How does the animal find food and water?
3. Describe the animal's habitat.

Use with page 33.

 0207.3.1

List Needs of Living Things

🕐 **in 5 minutes**

Materials: paper, pencil

1. Draw a picture of a plant or an animal.
2. Then list the things it needs that show it is a living thing.
3. Share your list with a classmate.

Use with page 58.

 0207.1.1

Express Lab

You Can...

Identify Rock Uses

🕐 **in 5 minutes**

Materials: magazines

1. Look through magazines for pictures of ways rocks are used. List what you see.
2. What ways did you see rocks being used?
3. **Communicate** Compare your list with a classmate. How are your lists different?

Use with page 85.

 0207.7.4

Use the Sun's Light to Change Paper

🕐 **in 5 minutes**

Materials: dark construction paper, solid classroom object

1. Put a piece of dark construction paper in a sunny spot.
2. Put a solid object on top of the paper.
3. Trace the object.
4. After five sunny days, remove the object. What happened to the paper?

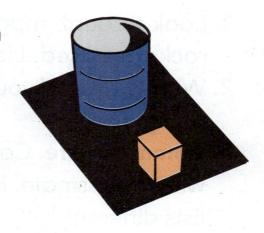

Use with page 104.

 0207.10.2

Express Lab
You Can...

Show Summer Weather

🕐 **in 5 minutes**
Materials: paper, pencil

1. Think of summer weather.
2. Think of what you like to do outside in summer.
3. Draw a picture of you having summer fun.
4. Why is summer a good time to do this activity?

Use with page 130.

Time a Change of State

⏱ **in 10 minutes**

Materials: ice cubes, plastic cup half full of room-temperature water, plastic cup half full of warm water, clock

1. Place one ice cube in room-temperature water and the other in the cup with warm water. This must be done at the same time.
2. Watch the clock and observe the ice cubes.
3. Record how long it took for the ice to change in each cup.
4. Compare what happened in each of the cups. Explain.
5. What states of matter did you observe?

Use with page 156.

 0207.9.2

Observe Sound

🕐 **in 5 minutes**

Materials: goggles, cardboard box, rubber band

1. **Safety:** Wear goggles. Stretch a rubber band around the box and over the open side.
2. Pluck the rubber band over the open side of the box. What happens?
3. **Infer** What caused the sound?

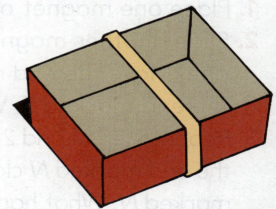

Use with page 173.

 0207.11.1

Observe Magnets

🕐 **in 5 minutes**
Materials: 2 bar magnets

1. Place one magnet on your desk.
2. Slide another magnet toward the first one. Move the end marked *N* close to the end marked *S*. What happens?
3. Repeat steps 1 and 2, but this time move the end marked *N* close to the end marked *N*. What happens?

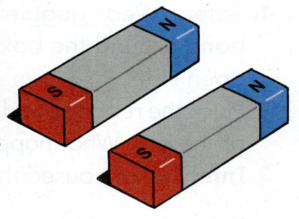

Use with page 192.

 0207.12.1

PHOTOGRAPHY CREDITS

KEY: (l) left, (r) right, (b) bottom, (t) top, (tl) top left, (tr) top right, (c) center, (cl) center left, (cr) center right, (bg) background, (bl) bottom left, (br) bottom right.

COVER: (Front) Darrell Gulin/Corbis; (Front-bg) NANCY ROTENBERG / Animals Animals-Earth Scenes; (Spine) Darrell Gulin/Corbis